Reaching Heaven

Reaching Heaven

DISCOVERING

t + H + e

CORNERSTONES

of Jesus'

PRayer Life

BRENDA POINSETT

© 2002 by
BRENDA POINSETT

ISBN: 0-8024-2297-7

1 3 5 7 9 10 8 6 4 2

Printed in the United States of America

To
Susan Miller
a faithful prayer
and
a loyal friend

contents

Acknowledgments 9
1. Lord, Teach Us to Pray 11

PART ONE: WITHDRAWAL

2. When You're Feeling Pressured 23
3. When You Need to Be Replenished 33
4. When You Have to Decide 45
5. When You Are Distracted 55
6. Am I Making an Impact? 65
7. When You Are Discouraged 75

PART TWO: THANKSGIVING

8. Recognizing the Ultimate Source 89
9. Thanks in Advance 101
10. The Trusting Side of Thanks 115

PART THREE: HONESTY

11. The Honest Struggle of a Troubled Heart 125
12. The Cup of Suffering 135
13. The Cry of Utter Loneliness 145

PART FOUR: INTERCESSION

14. The Cost of Intercession 159
15. The Power of Intercession 171
16. Interceding with Love 181
17. Perpetual Intercession 191
18. Magnanimous Intercession 201
Epilogue 211
Appendix 213
Bibliography 217

acknowLeDgments

I want to thank Moody Press, and Jim Bell in particular, for giving me the opportunity to write on Jesus' prayer life. It's an opportunity I wouldn't have wanted to miss. I love to study Jesus' life and share what I learn. I've written about Jesus' prayer life before, but there's always more to learn, and I wasn't disappointed.

Part of the learning came in dialoguing with others about what I studied. Sometimes this was in person and sometimes it was by e-mail. I'm grateful to Sandie Higley, John Melton, Mary Rose Fox, Chuck Fuller, David Gormong, Jay Latham, Jan Turner, Susan Miller, Margie Moore, Sandy Emmett, Pat Townsend, Janice Post, Debbie Hawkins, and my husband, Bob Poinsett, for their input, insight, and help. Some of these gave me permission to share their experiences in this book, which I appreciate.

Any project the magnitude of writing a book, no matter how stimulating, requires perseverance and discipline, and so I appreciate the prayers offered heavenward for me from Mary Rose Fox, Cookie Banderman, Susan Miller, Patty Molloy, Peggy Brooks, Jan Turner, and my husband. In the book I write about the power of intercession, and I experienced it while writing this book.

I also appreciate the editorial help I received from my husband, from Pat McAlister, and Moody's editorial team. What I learned from the study—what I wanted to convey—is clearer now because of their help.

One of the reasons Jesus chose the Twelve was so that they might be with Him. I can understand that. When you have a task to do, you need help, and I am truly grateful for all those who helped me write this book.

LORD, teach us to pray

While He was praying, heaven was opened, and the Holy Spirit descended upon Him in bodily form like a dove, and a voice came out of heaven, "Thou art My beloved Son, in Thee I am well-pleased."
—Luke 3:21–22 NASB 1977

Jesus' disciples had been with Him for over two years when they said, "Lord, teach us to pray" (Luke 11:1). At first glance, it is an odd request because they already knew how to pray. Their culture was immersed in prayer, so they were accustomed to praying. There were morning prayers and evening prayers. Prayers were offered at nine, twelve, three, and before meals. There were prayers for every occasion. No group of people ever had a higher ideal of prayer or ranked prayer higher in priorities than the Jews did.

But, as beautiful as these ideals were, faults crept in. The words fell glibly from their lips. The prayers for special occasions were observed without meaning. There was a tendency toward long prayers, as if men and women battered long enough at God's door, He would answer. They believed God could be talked—and even pestered—into concessions.

Likewise, faults may creep into our own praying.

Sometimes we may get in the rut of saying the same things over and over, or using tired worn-out phrases rather than saying what is really on our hearts.

Other times we're too quick about our praying. We pray on the run, or we pray with one eye closed and one eye on the clock.

We may lose our God-consciousness. We go through the motions, but we lose that sense of "You are here; You are responding; and I am listening."

We may fail to intercede for others; our prayers become a series of self-concerns. Or, maybe the opposite happens. We have a long list of people we are praying for and, consequently, fail to be personal and honest. We end up carrying burdens that we wouldn't have to carry.

It isn't as though we give these faults permission to enter our lives. Prayer is a discipline and is affected by life changes, new stresses, pressures, and disappointments. Consequently, our spiritual life suffers. In his classic work on prayer, Ole Hallesby said that prayer is the heartthrob of every believer.[1] When our prayer life isn't right, we rob our spiritual life of its vitality.

Because faults creep in, we need a role model, an inspiring example to pattern our prayer life after, someone to help us stay on track. I want that someone to be Jesus—don't you?

LEARNING FROM THE BEST

From time to time, we all pick role models to identify with and to imitate. This is one way we learn, grow, and change. Sometimes the selection process is unconscious; other times it is deliberate. For example, your parents may be your role model for parenting. You ended up parenting like them without giving it much thought. Or, you might have been like our friend Bob. When he found out his wife was pregnant, he said, "My eyes and ears opened, and I began noticing how parents interacted with their children. I saw what I wanted to imitate and what I didn't." That's how he learned his parenting skills.

We have many people we can learn about prayer from—biblical characters, great prayers such as George Müller and Rees Howell, fellow church members, friends, family members, and the authors of books. We have many possibilities for role models, but Jesus provides us a uniqueness that no other role model can, because He was both divine and human.

The Bible links answered prayer to praying in terms of God's will. As divine, Jesus knew perfectly the heart and mind of God. He can show us what to pray for, when to pray, and the kind of answers we can expect to receive. So much of Christian living—and of Christian praying—is wrapped up in knowing God's will. If I tallied the subjects of my prayers, more would have to do with discerning God's will than any other subject. How did Jesus' prayer life exemplify and reflect His understanding of God's will? And what can I learn from Him about claiming God's power to do His will? On three occasions, Jesus' prayers opened heaven. What is the secret to praying that will open heaven?

His divinity encourages me to pray because I want to know God's will, experience His power, and see heaven open, but His divinity may turn some people off. They would not consider Jesus a role model because they think of Him as having an insider's advantage. With a word He could heal people and cast out demons. He could produce food for multitudes and even change the weather. With power like that, why would anyone pray? Even if He did, His life was different from ours. We couldn't even begin to relate to Him, let alone imitate Him. What we need prayer help with is *life*: stress, pressures, temptations, and struggles.

The truth is that while Jesus was divine, He was also fully human. To suppose that His divinity freed Him from operating under the limitations that we do is to undermine the truth of John 1:14: "And the Word became flesh, and dwelt among us" (NASB). He was made like us, and nothing shows His humanity more than His prayer life. He knew the stress of having too much to do in too little time, the pressure of dealing with people, the intensity of temptation, and the struggle to submit to God's will.

Do you want to learn from someone who can show us the mind and heart of God while living under circumstances pretty much like ours? Do you want to learn from the best? If you do, I invite you to study Jesus' prayer life with me.

HOW WE WILL STUDY

When the disciples wanted to learn about prayer from Jesus, He was right there in their midst. All they had to do was ask, face-to-face. We don't have that same opportunity because Jesus is no longer here in the flesh, but we do have the biblical record to study and His Holy Spirit to teach us (John 14:26).

The biblical record is a bit of a challenge because we don't always know what He prayed for. At times His prayers are actually stated, but several times what He was praying about is inferred by the circumstances. Here our judgment will enter in. That is, we will determine the object of prayer by analyzing the incident, including what happened before Jesus prayed and what happened afterward. Let's look at Jesus' first recorded prayer to see how this works.

The incident. When John the Baptist come out of the wilderness preaching a baptism of repentance for forgiveness of sin (Luke 3:3), Jesus wanted to be baptized. John resisted because Jesus didn't need to repent. Jesus insisted, "It is proper for us to do this to fulfill all righteousness" (Matthew 3:15). He wanted to please God, and as He was baptized, He prayed, and three things happened (Luke 3:21–22).

1. Heaven opened, indicating that a revelation from God would follow.

2. The Holy Spirit, God's power, descended on Jesus "in bodily form like a dove."

3. A voice from heaven said, "Thou art My beloved
   Son, in Thee I am well-pleased" (NASB 1977).

Those last words were pregnant with meaning, as any con-
scientious Jew would have recognized. They were composed
of two texts from the Old Testament. "Thou art My beloved
Son" is from Psalm 2:7, and "in Thee I am well pleased" is part
of Isaiah 42:1.

"Thou art My Son" in Psalm 2:7 (NASB 1977) was always
accepted as a description of the messianic king. This messianic
psalm foretold the triumph of the Messiah, the anointed King
of God. "Behold, My Servant, whom I uphold; My chosen one
in whom My soul delights" (Isaiah 42:1 NASB 1977) is from a
description of the servant of the Lord whose portrait culminates
in the sufferings of One who was wounded for our transgres-
sions and bruised for our iniquities, the One on whom the chas-
tisement of our peace fell, the one who was to be like a sheep,
dumb before its shearers (see Isaiah 53).

What happened before. Before His baptism, Jesus was living at home, working as a carpenter in Nazareth. Scholars often
refer to those years before His baptism as "the silent years"
because the Bible gives so little information about them. We
have only His birth story (Luke 2:1–20) and His leaving Nazareth
when He was twelve to go with His parents to Jerusalem for
the Passover (Luke 2:41–50).

What happened afterward. After His baptism, Jesus' life
changed dramatically. He began preaching and teaching in
Judea. When He returned to Galilee, He did not return home
to Nazareth but established a ministry base in Capernaum.
"The silent years" become "the vocal years" as He taught and
preached.

Jesus' baptism was a line of demarcation with a clear
"before" and "after." Jesus' life turned from private to public;
He left His home and His carpenter's job and began His public ministry. At this pivotal point in His life, for what might
Jesus have been praying?

THE INFERENCE

Perhaps during those "silent years," Jesus pondered His unique relationship with God the Father and wondered what all it would involve. Just when Jesus knew His unusual destiny is hard to say. Surely He did not know it when He was a baby in the manger or as a small child. I can't imagine a three-year-old knowing He was the Son of God who would someday die on a cross for the salvation of men and women. His question to His parents in Jerusalem, when they thought He had been lost, indicates some awareness of who He was. He said, "Didn't you know I had to be in my Father's house?" (Luke 2:49). Nevertheless, He went back home as the obedient son, back to a life of family, worship, and business. While He hammered and sawed, He must have pondered what mission God had for Him to do. Would God want Him to speak to people? How would He speak? Scathing like the prophets of old? Or gentle and understanding? How would people receive His message? Would He be received? Or would He be opposed?

Some readers may be uncomfortable with the idea that Jesus would have asked these kinds of questions, and yet asking them is a normal part of maturing. If Jesus fully entered the human situation, then He had to grow into a consciousness of who He was, and He had to discover His mission. Luke said, "Jesus kept increasing in wisdom and stature, and in favor with God and men" (2:52 NASB); and the writer of Hebrews said, "Although He was a Son, He learned obedience from the things which He suffered. And having been made perfect, He became . . . the source of eternal salvation" (5:8–9 NASB).

The urgency of the questions, of needing to hear from God, prompted Him to leave home, go hear John the Baptist preach, and become a part of a movement where God was visibly working. As He was baptized, He prayed.

When He prayed, heaven opened, God revealed Himself. His Spirit fell on Jesus, empowering Him for ministry. God spoke words of affirmation—words that gave Jesus direction for His future. He was indeed to be the King sent by God, and this way would involve not power and glory but suffering and death. The way ahead was now clear, and it was time to start. The inference is that Jesus prayed because He needed to hear from God, He needed His power, and He needed direction. Do you have a need for those things in your life? If you do, then you will be able to connect with Jesus.

JESUS' NEED FOR PRAYER

If Christ had not felt the need to pray, He might seem to us, especially in the light of His sinlessness, an impressive and awesome figure, but He would not seem close to our lives. We need to pray, and we will learn more from Him when we acknowledge that He, too, needed to pray.

If we don't believe this—if we don't acknowledge His humanity—then we will miss an important point of connection. He will be like an actor on a far-off stage that we feel totally detached from. The tears, the sweat, the agony do not affect us. On the other hand, if Jesus needed to pray—if the stress, the pressure, and the struggles He experienced were real—then He no longer seems like an actor going through the motions on a far-off stage. We feel as though we are "in this together," and a kinship develops. *If He needed prayer, then we do too.* And this thought naturally leads to, *If He prayed this way, then perhaps we should too.* Identification and imitation go hand in hand.

Because we are more likely to imitate those with whom we feel a kindred spirit, Jesus reveals to us divine possibilities when we study His prayer life. For example, I can read a line that says He prayed at His baptism and be unmoved. But when I look at the fuller picture and see what He was possibly experiencing, I recognize that I hunger for prayer that opens heaven. I am prompted to pray because I need and want God's power and His direction. I can be more specific and confident in my praying, articulating my need because I know how Jesus prayed.

We can gain much by the process of drawing inferences about Jesus' unstated prayers. This doesn't mean, though, that

17

we don't need to look at the context of the other prayers, the ones where we actually have the words. Even then, for growth's sake, it is still a good idea to look at what was happening in His life. The fuller the understanding we gain of what He was experiencing, the greater the chances for identification and imitation.

To know what was happening when Jesus prayed, I used a harmony of the Gospels. The Gospel writers weren't concerned with a time sequence, so we need a tool that puts the events of Jesus' life in order of occurrence. A harmony synchronizes those events and arranges them in chronological order. In an appendix, I have listed Jesus' prayers in the order of their occurrence. To get a fuller picture, though, you might want to consult a harmony, available at libraries and Christian bookstores. The one I used for this study is *A Harmony of the Gospels for Students of the Life of Christ,* by A. T. Robertson (New York: Harper, 1922, 1950). You might want to take the list of Jesus' prayers and, using a harmony, draw your inferences and compare them with mine. You may come to agree with mine, and you may not. Either way, you will glean, gain, and grow, because you opened your spiritual eyes and ears to see a perfect role model.

Although I used a harmony to study the context of Jesus' prayers, we are not going to look at the prayers in this book in their chronological sequence. Rather, I've organized traits around the four outstanding characteristics of His prayer life because I think that makes it easier to imitate Him.

TRAITS TO CONNECT WITH

When we identify and imitate a role model, we don't usually imitate everything about the person at one time. We imitate dominant traits—traits that stand out to us, traits that we admire.

When I studied Jesus' prayer life, I spotted four prominent cornerstones. There were many lessons I could have drawn, but these stood out.

- *Jesus repeatedly withdrew for prayer.* Time alone with the Father was very important to Him.

- *Jesus laced His living with thanksgiving.* In good times, bad times, and challenging times, Jesus had a heart of gratitude.

- *Jesus was honest with God.* In His struggle with God's will, He felt no need for cover-up. He expressed what He felt.

- *Jesus interceded for others.* At the times of greatest pressure in His life, He still thought of others and prayed for them.

Because these were the prominent characteristics of His prayer life, they stayed with me, continually reminding me of the essentials I needed if I wanted a prayer life that opened heaven. I noticed that when I didn't practice these traits, my prayer life suffered. It was like what might happen to a building if you pulled out an important foundation stone. The building is still there; it still provides shelter, but it is weak and insecure. That's when I started labeling these traits the cornerstones of Jesus' prayer life. My "house of prayer" is weakened when a cornerstone is removed. I'm still praying but not with forcefulness and confidence.

The cornerstones of Jesus' prayer life are the foundation of the kind of prayer that opens heaven so God can respond to us, giving us His power and direction. They were indispensable to Jesus' prayer life, and the challenge before us is to make them indispensable to ours.

When we do, "our calling will become clearer, our work for God will become more powerful, our relationship to God will become more genuine, and possibly, we will hear God communicate back to us to commend us, even as God commended the First-born: 'With you I am well pleased.'"[2]

makin**g** the
CONNECTION

What can I gain by making the cornerstones of Jesus' prayer life the cornerstones of mine?

What is the difference between knowing Jesus struggled and believing He did?

Notes

1. Ole Hallesby, *Prayer*, trans. Clarence J. Carlsen (Minneapolis: Augsburg, 1994), 37.
2. William David Spencer and Aída Besançon Spencer, *The Prayer Life of Jesus: Shout of Agony, Revelation of Love, A Commentary* (Lanham, Md.: Univ. Press of America, 1990), 147.

PART ONE

withdrawal

WHEN YOU'RE
FEELING PRESSURED

The whole town gathered at the door, and Jesus healed many who had various diseases. He also drove out many demons. . . .
Very early in the morning, while it was still dark, Jesus got up, left the house and went off to a solitary place, where he prayed.
—Mark 1:33–35

How do you measure success? Is your definition often connected to size? A certain *amount* of money. A *large* house. A *wide* reputation. A *broad* influence. A *huge* following.

Even when we talk about churches or spiritual movements, we often use the size measure: If several thousand people are involved, then it must be a success. If you asked me if I agreed with that standard, I would say, "No, I don't," and yet I find myself judging events by size. When I return from a speaking engagement and Bob, my husband, asks how it went, it is not unusual for me to say how many attended or how many books were sold. It is hard not to use size as a measure.

By the size measurement, we would judge Jesus' ministry successful when His popularity exploded. That would be time to applaud, to rest on laurels, or to work to maintain momentum, yet Jesus had a different reaction—one that involved prayer. Let's see what that was.

EXPLODING POPULARITY

After His baptism in Judea, Jesus began His ministry there more or less in obscurity as people got acquainted with the stranger from Galilee. He enlisted some disciples, including Peter, Andrew, James, and John, and established Himself as a preacher. For a while, the ministries of Jesus and John the Baptist ran concurrently. After John was put in prison, Jesus went to Galilee, where He proclaimed the good news (Mark 1:14).

Jesus went to one of Galilee's populous cities, Capernaum. On the Sabbath, He taught in the synagogue (v. 21). Jesus amazed the people by the way He taught (v. 22). He wasn't like the scribes (the teachers of the law), who rehashed what others said and never gave their own opinions. When Jesus spoke, He spoke "with utter independence. He cited no authorities and quoted no experts. He spoke with the finality of the voice of God. To the people it was like a breeze from heaven to hear someone speak like that."[1]

Jesus' words amazed the people, but His deeds left them thunderstruck.

While He was teaching in the synagogue, a man possessed with an evil spirit created a disturbance. Jesus spoke sternly to the evil spirit. "'Be quiet! . . . Come out of him!' The evil spirit shook the man violently and came out of him with a shriek" (vv. 25–26).

No one had ever seen anything like this, even though they were used to exorcisms. The people believed strongly in unclean spirits; consequently, there were many exorcists who worked at casting out demons. The exorcists used elaborate incantations, spells, special formulas, and magical rites. But Jesus, with one sentence of authority, exorcised an evil spirit. The power was not in a spell, a formula, an incantation, or a magical rite; the power was Jesus, and the people were astonished. "What is this? A new teaching—and with authority! He even gives orders to evil spirits and they obey him" (v. 27). What a wonder! News about Jesus and His ability spread quickly (v. 28).

Immediately after the synagogue services, Jesus and His disciples went to Peter and Andrew's home. Peter's mother-in-law was ill with a fever. Jesus "went to her, took her hand and helped her up. The fever left her" (v. 31). No magical paraphernalia was used; no special recitations; with a simple gesture Jesus healed her.

Working wasn't permitted on the Sabbath, but talking was, and news of the miracle-worker in town spread quickly. What great publicity for an unknown rabbi, a newcomer to town! And it was effective. That evening after sunset—just as soon as the Sabbath ended—the whole town gathered to see Jesus. The people brought with them their hopes and expectations.

POPULARITY'S EXPECTATIONS

As the news spread of Jesus' unusual words and acts, so did hope. *Perhaps this new man in town can restore my father's sight. Maybe He can make our crippled daughter walk again! Oh, think of it! Maybe He can bring freedom to our neighbor who is tormented day and night by an evil spirit.*

With high hopes, the people brought to Jesus all who were ill and demon-possessed. "The whole town gathered at the door, and Jesus healed many who had various diseases. He also drove out many demons" (vv. 33–34). Jesus met their expectations. The people must have thought how great it would be to have someone like Jesus always around. *Here is the solution to all our ills! Wouldn't it be nice if He stayed in Capernaum? We would never again have to worry about our ill and tormented family members and friends. Cures would always be available. What security!*

The disciples, too, probably thought staying around would be a good idea. Judging by the numbers (the *whole* town gathered, and Jesus healed *many*), Jesus, their leader, was a success. *How thrilling to see so many people come to Jesus! We must be doing something right. This is a highly populated area, so let's work here where we can reach many people. We've got a good thing going; let's not mess with success.*

Jesus sensed their thoughts. He knew the people were going to try to keep Him from leaving. He realized they wanted to keep Him in their community, concerned about themselves only. Without their saying a word, He could sense the evaluation of the disciples about what had happened.

Their thoughts sparked thoughts of His own.

Should I go or should I stay? The people of Capernaum are needy; should I localize My ministry and stay here? It is a bustling city of many people. Wouldn't that be a large enough ministry area? Or, should I go to other areas?

The disciples deserve some consideration. Wouldn't a ministry in one place be better for them?

What about the spectacular healings? Are they consistent with the mission God has given Me? To be sure, they attract people, but will I be able to lead them on to deeper spiritual truths? Or, are they interested only in miracles?

Among the questions circulating in His thoughts was a greater—and more important—question, one directed toward His heavenly Father: *What do You want Me to do?*

FINDING THE ANSWER

At Jesus' baptism, God solidified for Him the direction for His life: He was to be the suffering Messiah. In the temptations that followed (Matthew 4:1–11; Luke 4:1–13), the broad principles of His ministry were hammered out. Considering who He was, you would think that would have been all He needed. He knew God's will; it was just a simple matter of doing it. Life, however, even for the Son of God, was not that simple.

Although Jesus knew the general direction and the broad principles for His life and ministry, He still needed God's guidance at various junctures. If that were not the case, Jesus would have been a mere robot or a puppet. Rather, He was a thinking person, a person who could be tempted, a person who interacted with people and was touched by their needs; therefore, He needed to consult God from time to time, and the incident at Capernaum was one of those times. The next morning "while it was still dark, Jesus got up, left the house and went off to a solitary place, where he prayed" (Mark 1:35).

the need for solitude

This is the first of several incidents that show Jesus' need for times of prayerful solitude. Withdrawing for communicating with the Father is the most obvious characteristic of His prayer life. On this particular occasion, He withdrew early in the morning.

The morning after the crowd had gathered the night before, Jesus left Peter and Andrew's home to find a solitary place where He could pray. I would like to think the time He chose is significant. I'm a morning person by nature; my best praying comes during the early morning before the rest of the household awakens and the outside and inside noises of life begin. Jesus, though, as we are going to see in future chapters, didn't always choose the same time of day for His withdrawals. More than likely He chose the early morning on this occasion because that was when He could get solitude. The crowds were there at the door of the house the night before. After everyone had departed, surely late because of the number wanting to be healed, there would have been pleasantries to exchange with His hosts. Early morning, before the household was awake and before the townspeople had time to regroup, Jesus sought a place where He could be alone, where He would not be distracted, where He could articulate His thoughts and commune with God without interruptions.

It was a good thing Jesus went early to a lonely place because the people weren't going to leave Him alone for long. When Peter and those with him awoke and discovered that Jesus had disappeared, they went searching for Him (Mark 1:36). When they spotted Jesus, they said, "Everyone is looking for you!" (v. 37).

When the townspeople found Jesus, they tried to keep Him from leaving their area (Luke 4:42), just as He had thought they would.

The time of solitude wasn't long, but it was sufficient. Decisively and firmly, Jesus said to Peter and his companions, "Let us go somewhere else—to the nearby villages—so I can preach there also. That is why I have come" (Mark 1:38).

Through prayerful solitude, Jesus came to understand clearly God's direction at this time. He must leave the miracle-seeking multitude and go to other places. By the time Peter and the others arrived, Jesus had His answer: "Go somewhere else" (v. 38). Capernaum was a starting point, not an ultimate goal. He could declare what He was going to do because He had prayed. His prayer had reached heaven, and God had responded; therefore, Jesus left Capernaum and traveled throughout Galilee, preaching in synagogues and driving out demons (v. 39).

Can you identify with Jesus? Do you have times when the expectations of others press in against you and you become confused? Or, times when God's will just isn't as clear as you would like? When you wonder about God's specific will in a particular situation, it may be a signal that you need to imitate Jesus by spending time alone in quiet communion with God.

Jesus needed lonely places, without the presence of people and their continual interruptions, to seek God's guidance, and so do we. Solitude reduces distractions, facilitates thinking, and improves our listening ability.

Reduces distractions. People, even when it is just one or two, are distracting for most of us. Even when they don't mean to be, they can still be a distraction.

There are just two of us at our house; my husband works outside the home and I work at home. When he decides to work at home, I bristle at the thought of my early morning solitude being interrupted. If I say as much, Bob protests, "But it's my home too."

I'll say, "Yes, I know, but . . . ," thinking of how one small request, a cough, or a sneeze can interrupt my focus.

He promises to be quiet, and he is, but I will hear him when he searches for something in the basement. *Hmm. I wonder what he is looking for.* I try to ignore it. I hear doors slamming. *What could it be?* More noise. I open the basement door and say, "May I help you find something?"

Perhaps he'll tiptoe into the kitchen, which is next to my office where I am praying. He fixes himself a piece of toast. I smell it, look at the clock, and wonder if it isn't time for a snack.

When my children were home, I gladly prayed with many distractions because solitude was hard to come by. One of the perks, though, of the empty nest is quality solitude, which I prefer for times when I really need my prayers to reach heaven. To hear from God, I need to give Him my undivided attention.

Other people aren't the only distraction; sometimes it is what is going on inside us, and solitude will help us deal with that too.

Facilitates thinking. Our "to do" list may be a distraction, although it makes no noise that can be measured in decibels. The distraction is the internal pressure that says, "You've got so much to do. You don't have time to pray." Even a daily quiet time can become another item to check off of our "to do" list. We can have a brief devotional reading and say our prayers, and still keep one eye on the clock. This is not to say that our agendas are not important, but for prayerful times to discern God's will, we must sort out what we are thinking, let our breathing slow, relax in and acknowledge God's presence, and listen for His voice.

You often hear people say, "I just need to be alone with my thoughts." Solitude provides an environment that will enable us to sort out what is bothering us, identify the pressures we are experiencing, and examine our feelings. When we do this, we are better able to articulate our need to God.

Many of us live in households where televisions, radios, telephones, and computer games create a constant buzz that makes thinking difficult.

For others, it may be inner voices that are bothering us. We may be bombarded by swirling thoughts of anxiety or negativity. The thoughts and their intensity will vary depending on the individual and the circumstances.

Reducing the buzz of televisions and radios can be accomplished by turning them off, if you have that kind of power in your household. Turning off inner noise can be somewhat more difficult. Here are three things I do to help with this.

1. *Keep a note pad and pencil handy when I pray.* When those intruding thoughts of *You need to get that letter in the mail today,* or, *Don't forget to pay the electric bill* enter my head, I jot them down. When I do this, I can let go of the intruding thought. Because I've written it down, I know I won't forget it.

2. *Write in a journal about complicated issues.* When I write down my inner distracting thoughts, they lose their intensity. I can identify troubling emotions and pressures when I look at what I've written. This improves my ability to articulate my needs.

3. *Verbally confess frustrations.* Sometimes I do the sorting out and identifying as a part of my dialogue with God. "Father, I am in Your presence this morning. I recognize that You are here. I know You have a will for my life. I'm having a hard time figuring out exactly what that is. Maybe it is my own confusion and anxiety. Here is what is bothering me . . ."

When we sort out what we are feeling during times of solitude, it improves our ability to listen to God, and that is the most important thing when we are seeking God's specific will.

Improves our listening ability. When we want to connect with God in a way that we will hear Him speak, we need a spirit-to-Spirit connection. For this to happen, "there must be that profound and wondrous 'quiet' wherein it is possible to be aware of the 'still small voice' of God's gracious Spirit."[3]

- In a cave apart from the masses of people and away from the wrath of Jezebel, Elijah heard the "still small voice" of God (1 Kings 19:8–12 KJV; "a gentle whisper," NIV).

- Moses was tending sheep in a deserted mountainous area when He heard God speak through a burning bush (Exodus 3:1–6).

- Paul went off to the Arabian desert after his conversion to make a decision about what God wanted him to do with his life (Galatians 1:15–17).

If we want the specifics of God's will, we will need to be quiet enough to hear Him speak, and we will want to make sure we hear what He says because His answers may challenge us.

In light of the success Jesus was experiencing, it looks as if the rational, reasonable answer would have been, "Stay right where You are. Call a press conference. You can get more publicity out of this. You not only have the record of exorcisms and miraculous healings, but look at the size of the crowd. Word will spread. People will come to You from all over. Look how My name will be glorified."

But God said—and Jesus heard—"It's time to go on to minister in other places." There is a very real sense in which this is a directive for all of us. "We must go on to the next stage in our religious experience. We must keep our minds and hearts in motion. We must push on to the next task . . . [to] new people into whose lives we may bring some of the good news of God's kingdom."[4] Obedience is always current, so we need to be continually seeking times of prayerful solitude to discern exactly what it is God wants us to do.

To learn the specifics of God's will, we may have to be just as deliberate and persevering as Jesus was. The people who pursued Him were very aggressive, so Jesus got up "very early" and "while it was still dark" to find a solitary place. This indicates decisiveness; it takes effort to get up early while it is still dark. Can we leave the warmth of the bed, the comfort of our lifestyle, the familiarity of the sounds in our life, and the pressures to succeed so that we can seek out a lonely place where we can hear His voice?

makinɡ the
CONNECtION

Why is morning a good time for prayerful solitude?

What distracts me the most when I withdraw for prayer?

Notes

1. William Barclay, *The Gospel of Mark,* 2d ed., The Daily Study Bible (Edinburgh: Saint Andrew, 1956, 1964), 24.
2. Implied by the exclamation in Mark 1:37.
3. W. Phillip Keller, "Solitude for Serenity and Strength," *Decision,* August-December 1981, 8.
4. *The Interpreter's Bible* (Nashville: Abingdon, 1955), 7:666.

WHEN YOU
NEED TO BE
REPLENISHED

Yet the news about him spread all the more, so that crowds of people came to hear him and to be healed of their sicknesses. But Jesus often withdrew to lonely places and prayed.

—Luke 5:15–16

When Jesus healed the sick and demon possessed in Capernaum, no mention was made of anyone's being healed of leprosy (Mark 1:32, 34). Perhaps it is implied in "He healed many who were ill with various diseases" (v. 34 NASB), but maybe not. Leprosy was thought to be highly contagious, so once a diagnosis was made, a leper was banished from society. They were untouchables. People wouldn't have gathered up their leprous family members and brought them to Jesus because they were terrified of the horribly disfiguring disease. This didn't keep a leper, though, from approaching Jesus. Word about Jesus' phenomenal works must have reached his ears, for "when he saw Jesus, he fell with his face to the ground and begged him, 'Lord, if you are willing, you can make me clean'" (Luke 5:12). It was a request that would take Jesus' popularity—and His prayer life—to a new level.

too good to keep

After Jesus left Capernaum, He preached and healed in other Galilean cities, and it was in one of those towns that the leper approached Him. The Bible describes him as "covered with leprosy" (Luke 5:12) or "full of leprosy" (NASB 1977), meaning he had a very serious case. The leper approached Jesus with confidence; he had heard enough about Jesus to know He could heal him. He didn't demand to be healed; he only said, "If you want to, you can make me clean."

"Jesus reached out his hand and touched the man. 'I am willing,' he said. 'Be clean!' And immediately the leprosy left him" (Luke 5:13).

"Jesus sent him away at once with a strong warning: 'See that you don't tell this to anyone. But go, show yourself to the priest and offer the sacrifices that Moses commanded for your cleansing'" (Mark 1:43–44).

I can understand Jesus' wanting the cured leper to show himself to the priest. It was his ticket back into society according to the Law of Moses (Leviticus 13–14). "After showing the priest indications of healing and making an offering of thanksgiving, the healed leper would cleanse his body, change his clothes, and become an accepted part of society again." [1]

Harder to understand is Jesus' telling the cured man not to tell. How could you not tell that you had been healed of a loathsome disease? I remember once when a man broke into our house very early on a Sunday morning and caused quite a ruckus. Later, when we left for church, my husband said to our sons, "Now don't say anything about this to anyone." I was glad he didn't say that to me! I wouldn't have been able to keep quiet. There are some things you've got to tell. Being healed from leprosy would be right at the top. I would have been just as disobedient as the healed leper. He "began to talk freely, spreading the news" (Mark 1:45).

Those he told, told others. Stories of any miraculous healing spreads fast, but a story of a leper being healed spread like wildfire. This particular story would quickly be told and retold because it had interesting details—the kind of details that make listeners gasp, "He did *what?*"

THE DARING JESUS

Jesus touched a leper, something everyone avoided. Lepers went around shouting "Unclean! Unclean!" so that no one would even accidentally touch them.

In the eyes of the people, Jesus risked infection and becoming ceremonially defiled by touching the man. The medical knowledge of that day considered leprosy highly contagious.

The Jewish law said you must not touch a leper. If you did, you became ceremonially defiled, which meant social and religious exclusion. Jesus touched him anyway. He risked becoming ceremonially defiled to minister to human need, something the religious leaders would never have done. They were displeased and disgusted by Jesus' actions.

Likewise, they were upset with Jesus for pronouncing the leper clean in Luke 5:13. Only the priest in the temple in Jerusalem was supposed to do that. If the news of this cure got into the hands of the right people, Jesus would be in trouble. He would be proclaimed a revolutionist and accused of being disloyal to the Jewish law.

Even though told not to tell, the cured leper told others this story with the delicious tidbits; in turn, they told still more people, and Jesus' popularity skyrocketed.

THE STORY'S EFFECT

The spreading of the story of the leper's healing increased Jesus' popularity, taking it to a new level. It wasn't *a* crowd anymore who gathered to hear Him and be healed of their diseases, it was "crowds" (Luke 5:15). The *New American Standard Bible* (1977) translates it as "great multitudes . . . gathering to hear Him and to be healed of their sicknesses." Mark describes them as coming from everywhere (Mark 1:45).

What an opportunity to heal and to help many people! The people were present; their needs were evident. We would expect Jesus to keep the momentum going, but instead He withdrew. He went to the wilderness and prayed (Luke 5:16). He needed rest, refreshment, and fortification.

Rest. A person with a severe hearing loss said, "We live in a noisy world, where people are always talking or listening to the radio, stereo, or TV. When I remove my hearing aid at the end of the day, I am surrounded by total silence—a silence that hearing people seldom experience. This silence is soothing and relaxing. It renews the spirit."[2]

Jesus connected solitude with rest. When so many people were clamoring around them that Jesus and the disciples didn't even have time to eat, Jesus said, "Come away by yourselves to a secluded place and rest a while" (Mark 6:31 NASB).

When the crowds gathered after the healing of the leper, Jesus went to the wilderness, which means an uninhabited region. As we saw in the last chapter, solitude reduces distractions, facilitates thinking, and improves listening. These are all very important to praying that reaches heaven, but solitude also provides rest, which is important too. The press of the crowds was so great that "Jesus could no longer enter a town openly but stayed outside in lonely places" (Mark 1:45) to pray and to unwind and recover. Still, the people wouldn't leave Him alone. They came to Him "from everywhere" (v. 45c), and they came to Him with needs.

Refreshment. To really help people, there must be an identification with the sufferer. Jesus was deeply moved[3] at the plight of the leper. Jesus reached out and touched him before the healing ever took place. The most terrible thing about being a leper was the isolation it brought. With sensitivity to his pain, Jesus touched Him. Oh, what that touch must have meant to the untouchable!

In a Bible study once, a person tried to convince me that the reason Jesus healed was a gimmick to draw people to Him.

If that were the case, Jesus wouldn't have had to withdraw to recuperate. "Every time Jesus healed anyone it took something out of Him."[4] Matthew, in quoting Isaiah, said of Jesus, "He took up our infirmities and carried our diseases" (Matthew 8:17). When the woman with the hemorrhage of blood touched Jesus, He said, "I was aware that power had gone out of Me" (Luke 8:46 NASB).

In order to respond to the needy who flocked to Him, Jesus had to separate himself from time to time so "that through communion with his Father the reservoirs of his own soul might be filled again from the fountains that were on high."[5] You can't always be giving out unless you are sometimes taking in.

Fortification. One reason Jesus may have ordered the healed leper to keep quiet was because He did not want to attract attention and create a stir. God's people were subservient to the Romans who were in power. They dreamed of a day when a divine deliverer would come. "But for the most part they dreamed of that day in terms of military conquest and political power. For that reason Palestine was the most inflammable country in the world. It lived amidst revolutions. Leader after leader arose, and had his moment of glory and was then eliminated by the might of Rome."[6]

Now, with the increasing popularity that Jesus was experiencing because of His power to do supernatural things, the people might want to install Him as their political leader and a military commander, yet Jesus had to help them "to see that His power was love and not force of arms. He had to work almost in secrecy until men knew Him for what He was, the lover and not the destroyer of the lives of men."[7]

Another reason Jesus might have been concerned about the crowds was the developing opposition against Him. Talk of great crowds, phenomenal acts, and religious rule-breaking raised their ire. Jesus had left Judea months ago because of what the Pharisees in Jerusalem were saying about Him (John 4:1–2). Jesus' concern was well founded. When He returned to Capernaum after the leper's healing, people gathered around Him, and in the crowd were Pharisees and teachers of the Law (scribes) "who had come from every village of Galilee and Judea and from Jerusalem" (Luke 5:17 NASB). "This is the first account of the organized opposition of the Scribes and Pharisees in Galilee."[8]

When Jesus touched the leper, He knowingly was risking ceremonial pollution. When He pronounced him clean, something only a priest should have done, He was courting criticism. When the crowds swelled around Him, the door opened to religious criticism. Once opened, it would not close. From here on out, Jesus would be under the scrutiny of hostile and critical eyes. It was something He was going to have to steel Himself to face, which is why He needed to pray.

In prayerful solitude, "The love in the eyes of God comforted Him for the hate in the eyes of men. The approval of God nerved Him to meet the criticism of men."[9]

For the battles ahead—resisting the people's desire for a military leader and dealing with the opposition—Jesus prepared with prayer, and it probably wasn't just a one-time prayer.

HABITUAL WITHDRAWING

So far we have interpreted the prayer mentioned in Luke 5:16 as a specific time of prayer. Actually the verse as it is translated in some versions of the Bible implies a pattern.

- "But Jesus Himself would often slip away to the wilderness and pray" (NASB).
- "But Jesus often withdrew to lonely places and prayed" (NIV).
- "But he would go away to lonely places, where he prayed" (TEV).

The impression is more of a habitual pattern than a single act. This doesn't take anything away from what we have already said about what Jesus might have prayed following the healing of the leper. If there were a pattern, there would still have been this specific incident of prayer.

Not only this incident but many others show that Jesus repeatedly withdrew for prayer. One-third of this book is devoted to Jesus' need to be alone to pray. While the crowds continued to gather around Him day after day, Jesus slipped away from them from time to time. Jesus left needy people in order to engage in prayer, not because He did not care, but because He had to have times apart for rest, refreshment, and fortification. Most of us need times apart for the same reasons.

Rest from activity. We may be on a treadmill that just keeps going and going with activities—church meetings to attend, children or grandchildren to look after, gifts to buy, bills to pay, board meetings to attend, friends to keep up with. We long for rest, but expectations haunt us, spurring us on. We just keep going and going, "running on tired" as one of my friends puts it.

Refreshment for our souls. In his book *A Physician's Witness to the Power of Shared Prayer,* Dr. William F. Haynes writes about how draining difficult cases can be. "The stress is incalculable! When physicians have this much stress at work year in and year out, they have a great need for quiet, reflection, restoration, and a sense of peace daily . . . in order to maintain any sense of composure."[10]

Fortification for doing God's will. Just as Jesus felt the pull of societal pressures, we too may experience pressures to conform, to be someone other than who we believe God has called us to be. We need a strong resolve to be a person of integrity in a society filled with temptations.

These are ongoing concerns, and so we have an ongoing need for prayerful solitude, but where and when can we find it?

THE SOLITUDE CHALLENGE

Those with a natural bent toward solitude may find it easy to schedule moments for prayer in their lives. Those like me, with an empty nest, have an advantage now, but it wasn't always this way. I was reminded of this recently when a mother of a three-year-old and a four-month-old said to me, "I often feel like my relationship with God is on hold because I rarely have any alone time."

Another empty nester found just the opposite of my experience to be true because she embarked on a new career after her children left home. She said, "I feel so energized, so optimistic, so grateful for the opportunity to be able to move into this next phase of my life that it is intoxicating at times. I know I am doing what God has called me to do, yet I find it harder and harder to take time for being alone with God."

Gary, a high volume salesman working on commission, insists he can't find a place where everything stops so he can pray. He said, "Faxes are coming in, mail is arriving, the phone is ringing, e-mail messages are piling up. If I take time out, I will only get further behind."

The question is, Do we really believe prayerful solitude is beneficial? If we do, then we will have to work at finding solitude. The people who pursued Jesus were very aggressive. They seemed to have an uncanny sense for knowing where He was and how to find Him. They were ever present with their many needs—needs I'm sure Jesus didn't want to ignore; although at times, He did. We may have to be just as determined. Here's how three people discovered places for solitude.

1. John, a sensitive Christian and father of four young children, gets very innovative in finding time for solitude, such as in the car on the way to work or a blanket on the warm earth in the backyard after the children are in bed. When he has to go out of town for business, which is frequent, he arranges to arrive early. Before the conference begins, he will have a morning or afternoon of solitude in his hotel room or on the beach.

2. Whereas John deliberately searched for ways to be alone, Harold insisted he couldn't find the time because he had too much to do. Quite by accident, he discovered he had opportunity to be alone. When the time changed in the fall, Harold forgot to change his clock because he was helping a neighbor until nearly midnight. Consequently, he arrived at church an hour early. Not wanting to drive back home and then back again, he went into the sanctuary. As he sat in the quiet, he relaxed. He studied the stained glass window of Jesus, the gentle shepherd cuddling lambs. The tenderness of the scene touched Harold. Suddenly he sensed God's love enveloping him, and he began to pray. From then on, Harold went to church early to sit in the quiet sanctuary and pray. It became his appointed time with God.

3. Earlene wanted that kind of quiet, but she wanted it more often than once a week. At her house, something was always on. Her husband was a news junkie who turned on the radio the minute he got up. Her two teenagers were always playing music. Sometimes two boom boxes and one radio were playing at the same time. Maybe if her job wasn't so high-pressured, she could have prayed with the distractions, but she craved a time when everything shut down. When her pleas for "turn it off" went unheeded, she started getting up at four in the morning. She fixed herself some coffee, went on the balcony of their high-rise apartment, and watched the sun come up. Before the city was awake, before her family was awake, her soul awakened and was revitalized through prayerful solitude.

"We must make a lonely place. Nothing that enriches and empowers life ever just 'happens.' It is made. Jesus never 'happened' to find himself alone. He went out to put a stout fence around some corner of time and space,"[11] and so must we if we want solitude that provides rest, refreshment, and fortification.

makinς the
connection

Where are some lonely places I can use to seek rest, refreshment, and fortification?

What steps can I take to visit those places?

Notes

1. Ray Summers, *Commentary on Luke* (Waco, Tex.: Word, 1972), 64.

2. A writer in an Ann Landers column, *Sunday Herald-Times*, Bloomington, Ind., 9 July 1995, 4F.

3. See Mark 1:41.

4. William Barclay, *The Gospel of Mark*, 2d ed., The Daily Study Bible (Edinburgh: Saint Andrew, 1956, 1964), 131.

5. *The Interpreter's Bible*, (Nashville: Abingdon, 1955), 8:104.

6. William Barclay, *The Gospel of Matthew*, 2d ed., Vol. 1, The Daily Study Bible (Edinburgh: Saint Andrew, 1958, 1964), 304.

7. Ibid.

8. J. W. Shepard, *The Christ of the Gospels: An Exegetical Study* (Grand Rapids: Eerdmans, 1956), 138.

9. William Barclay, *The Gospel of Mark*, 3d ed., The Daily Study Bible (Edinburgh: Saint Andrew, 1956, 1964), 58.

10. William F. Haynes Jr., *A Physician's Witness to the Power of Shared Prayer* (Chicago: Loyola Univ. Press, 1990), 49.

11. *The Interpreter's Bible*, 7:104.

WHEN YOU
HAVE TO
DECIDE

[The scribes and the Pharisees] were filled with rage, and discussed together what they might do to Jesus.

It was at this time that He went off to the mountain to pray, and He spent the whole night in prayer to God. And when day came, He called His disciples to Him and chose twelve of them, whom He also named as apostles.
—Luke 6:11–13 NASB

Choices aren't always easy to make, even for Christians. Choices are sometimes agonizing because we want to do what is right. We want very much to please God, and we don't want regrets over "the road not taken."

Our choice may be about a crucial issue with heavy stakes. It may be about something less serious but still important to us. It may be a choice you've been thinking about making for some time, or it may be something you hadn't expected, such as a job offer. Do you stay with the job you know and like? Or do you take the risk of a new challenge?

Other times we might not have a choice before us that is well defined; we may be dealing with a situation in which we know that something needs to be done, but what? We may see no alternatives, or we may see too many and agonize over which road to take.

Turning points come to all of us when we must decide, Which way now? Or, what should I do? Or, how do I handle this? Such a turning point came for Jesus when a crisis developed in Jesus' ministry as the opposition against Him intensified.

a DEVELOPING CRISIS

The task of being the Messiah included showing what God really wanted in the way of worship and obedience. Religion for many Jews had become a matter of rules and regulations. Nowhere was this more true than in the observance of the Sabbath.

Honoring the seventh day of the week by not working "had developed into a very complicated and burdensome chore. The Mosaic restrictions had been elaborated and multiplied until they numbered into the hundreds."[1] Those oral restrictions made the keeping of the Sabbath practically impossible. What's more, they destroyed the spirit of the Sabbath (Mark 2:23–27).

Jesus could not tolerate the unnumbered and ridiculous regulations. "Real religion meant more than the observance of these regulations."[2] Jesus openly challenged the system, even healing a man whose condition could have waited until another day.

Jesus had entered the synagogue and was teaching. Among those gathered was a man whose right hand was withered. Also present were some scribes and Pharisees. They were watching Jesus closely to see if He would heal this man on the Sabbath. According to the oral law, healing was prevented on the Sabbath. It was all right to save a life but not to do anything that promoted healing.

Jesus knew their thoughts (Luke 6:8) and was angry about their callous disregard for the welfare of a fellow human being. He was "grieved at their hardness of heart" (Mark 3:5 NASB). Now, the man with the withered hand was not in grave danger; his life was not at stake. Jesus could have avoided the wrath of the scribes and the Pharisees by asking the man to come back another day. He could have asked the man to meet Him after sundown when the Sabbath was over. Instead, He asked him to come forward.

Jesus said to the scribes and Pharisees, "I ask you, is it lawful to do good or to do harm on the Sabbath, to save a life or to destroy it?" (Luke 6:9 NASB).

"After looking around at them all"—and I can imagine what a penetrating gaze that was—He said to the man, "'Stretch out your hand!' And he did so; and his hand was restored" (vv. 10–11 NASB).

To the religious leaders, this act was an affront to what they held sacred, and it wasn't the first time Jesus had challenged the Sabbath rules (Matthew 12:1–8; Mark 2:23–28; Luke 6:1–5; John 5:1–18). The scribes and Pharisees were filled with rage at what Jesus had done; seeing Jesus as a serious threat, they began discussing among themselves what they would do to Him (Luke 6:11). They even entered into what was for them an "unholy alliance" with the Herodians, a group who supported "Roman domination, followed the heathen customs, and held that Herod the Great was the Messiah."[3] Together they made plans to kill Jesus (Mark 3:6).

The dangers for Jesus were increasing daily. Already, in Nazareth an attempt had been made on His life. There He had been hustled to the hilltop in order to be hurled down but had escaped (Luke 4:29). This desire to see Him killed reminded Jesus that His time for accomplishing His mission on earth was limited.

a crucial choice

Jesus was aware as well that His mission was limited by space. There was so much Jesus wanted to say, to teach, and to do. If only He could reach people in more places! But He could be in only one place at a time. And in that day, with no means of mass communication, His voice could reach only a limited number of people. If a message was presented to people, it was presented personally. If Jesus' work was to branch out—and go on—Jesus needed helpers; He needed preachers to spread His message and to guarantee its existence after He was gone. His "general ministry to multitudes here and there must be supplemented by an organization that would give strength to his movement and guarantee its existence."4

For this, Jesus needed men who would commit themselves to Him. Jesus had many followers, but what He needed were men who would be loyal to Him, who would try to understand His purpose and task, and who would be willing to help Him carry it out. Out of His followers, He had to choose men on whose hearts and lives He could write His message and who would go out from His presence to carry that message abroad. Who would these men be?

Elton Trueblood called this decision to select the apostles one of the crucial decisions of the world. "There is no reason to suppose that we should ever have heard of the gospel apart from this carefully conceived step. Without this step the teaching of Christ might easily have been"5 a bubble which eventually burst. Gamaliel, a respected Pharisee, told about two bubbles that did eventually burst. He told of two would-be messiahs who were killed and whose work did not continue (Acts 5:36–37). If this were not to happen to the work of Jesus, He needed men to carry on His teachings. So, His choice of *who* those men would be was indeed a crucial one.

The choice was so crucial that it had to be faced in long hours of effort in order to know whom to select. The way Jesus handled it was through prayer. "He went off to the mountain to pray, and He spent the whole night in prayer to God" (Luke 6:12 NASB).

off to the mountain

In contrast with the last two incidents of withdrawal we looked at, Jesus chose to pray on a mountain this time. There is no way of knowing exactly where this mountain was, probably somewhere near the Sea of Galilee. Neither do we know if the mountain location had specific appeal for Him or was simply a convenient place to pray.

Where we pray can enhance our experience. For example, if I have a choice when I pray, I like to pray where I can view God's handiwork. God witnesses to me through His creation. Looking at stately oak trees from my deck, I often begin my prayers paraphrasing words of Jeremiah, "Ah, Sovereign Lord, You have made the heavens and the earth—this beautiful earth that I look at this morning. You did this by Your great power and outstretched arm. Nothing is impossible for You, and I know that none of the things I ask You today are beyond Your ability. You have shown Your love to thousands and You've certainly have shown it to me" (see Jeremiah 32:17–18).

Mountains were often places for communion with God (Exodus 19:24; 24:1–2; compare 32:1; also Numbers 27:12–23; compare 20:23–29). Climbing a mountain or hill and taking in the view from the heights adds to the spiritual experience. Climbing, going from a lower level to a higher level, helps us to disengage ourselves from problems and gives us a clearer mind to communicate with God. The view from the mountaintop facilitates our ability to gain God's perspective. In Jesus' case, spending the night on the mountain might have aided His communion with God. As the sun went down and the stars came out, He may have felt especially close to God and reminded of His power.

As much as I would like to believe Jesus chose the mountain because of its natural setting, He might have chosen it because it was what was available. He was dependent on others for hospitality; He didn't have a room of His own. A mountain may have given Him a place apart from distractions so that He could fully concentrate on the decision He had to make.

Either way, the text indicates that the only reason Jesus took the trouble to climb that mountain was to pray. Jesus did not go out for a hike up the mountain and then decide it would be nice to pray. His withdrawal to the mountain to pray all night reflected the burden that He carried. Alone and apart from all the distractions of the world below, Jesus sought illumination and guidance about the future of His ministry.

the white heat of prayer

This choice was so crucial that Jesus spent the "whole night" in prayer (Luke 6:12 NASB). The Greek word translated "whole night" is a medical term. It was used to describe the all-night vigil of a doctor as he waited at the bedside of a patient. The original word gives a "picture of urgency, earnestness, and intensity,"[6] reminding us of the work involved in prayer. It looks like a very simple "God, what would you have me to do?" would be answered immediately, but frequently it takes dialogue, verbalization, waiting, and listening to receive God's answer.

I can't imagine Jesus petitioning God with words all night long. As He considered the urgency of His need, I'm sure part of His prayer work was weighing the alternatives before Him.

Because we know He chose Simon Peter, Andrew, James, John, Philip, Bartholomew, Matthew, Thomas, James the son of Alphaeus, Simon the Zealot, Judas the son of James, and Judas Iscariot, we don't usually think about Jesus having alternatives, but He did. Many consider the number He chose to be symbolic, linking the apostles to the twelve tribes of Israel, connecting Jesus as the Messiah with a reconstituted Israel. But even that concept had to come to Jesus. Had He considered other possibilities? Maybe He considered seven because it was the perfect number or because a smaller group would have been easier to travel with.

Somewhere in that long prayer vigil, when the concept of the Twelve came to Him, the next question was, Who would those Twelve be? Out of all His disciples, which would be willing to identify his life with His? The crowds might be there one day and gone the next. Followers might fluctuate and be spasmodic in their attachment to Jesus, but He needed helpers who were dependable. Which ones would be faithful over the long haul? Who would be willing to travel and to be homeless? Which ones were courageous enough to identify with a rebel? Jesus was branded a sinner and a heretic; the opposition was determined to get Him. They would have to be courageous just to travel with Him.

As He considered the alternatives and their consequences, He listened. This is one reason we need time when we seek God's will so we can hear God responding, leading us along, directing our thinking, illuminating the situation, and bringing new thoughts to our mind. Indeed, Elton Trueblood once referred to this activity as "the white heat of prayer."[7] In this environment, "ideas fuse to form new unities, when they cannot fuse in colder environments."[8] In a vigil of prayer, we give God a warm environment for illuminating our choice and guiding us.

By morning, Jesus had the answer He needed. He called His disciples to Him, "And He appointed twelve, so that they would be with Him and that He could send them out to preach, and to have authority to cast out the demons" (Mark 3:14–15 NASB). Through prayer Jesus made a choice that enabled His ministry to expand beyond the limitations of space and time.

time for dialogue

Jesus went to a mountain for His all-night prayer vigil (Luke 6:12). For those of us who don't have access to a mountaintop (isolated natural area), we may have to look for another place to maintain our vigil. Although we see Jesus going to the wilderness and to the mountain, He also told us to use a room of prayer (Matthew 6:6). He was speaking of an inner room, of course, and even there He instructs, "When you have shut your door, pray" (Matthew 6:6 NASB 1977). Maintaining a vigil of prayer is about blocking out distractions so that we can focus on communicating with the Father, something we've already learned that solitude facilitates.

Maintaining a vigil doesn't necessarily mean spending one night in prayer, but it does mean spending *time* alone in prayer. Some of us with babies to tend to, children to watch, or jobs to keep may have to give God several chunks of time instead of maintaining one long vigil of prayer. In these chunks of time, we can continually bring before Him the choices we're facing.

Those chunks need to be long enough to allow for unhurried dialogue—speaking, listening, waiting, and receiving until we have God's answer. We need to pray about our decision until we have the inner assurance Jesus did. He prayed until He knew "This is the way, walk in it" (Isaiah 30:21 NASB). This is an answer worth waiting for!

I remember one occasion in which my husband and I were facing a choice about church membership. We were not members of the church we were attending. We had gone there to heal from a stressful situation in a denominational church where we were members. Although we didn't officially join the new congregation, we felt accepted and loved. But after we healed, Bob and I were convicted that we ought to resolve the matter of church membership. Do we join the church we are attending but which is not affiliated with our denomination? Do we return to our denomination? If so, what church? Do we go back to the church we left? Do we find another denominational church? We began making it a matter of prayer.

A young couple affiliated with our denomination moved to our city to start a new church. When they invited us to attend, we wondered if this was God's answer. When we attended, the attendance was so small that it didn't even feel like church. We were pretty pessimistic about the chances for the congregation's surviving. Nevertheless, we continued to pray, waiting for God's "This is the way, walk in it" answer. We visited other churches. We even tried the mission church again. By this time, they had moved from meeting in a school to a storefront building, but it still didn't seem to be a right fit.

After praying about this for several months, we took a trip. On the way home, Bob went to sleep, and I drove. In the quiet, I picked up the prayer vigil. Quietly, I talked to the Lord and listened for His response. I went over everything—the alternatives, consequences, reasons. And in the quiet, God's answer came as clear as a bell: Join the mission church. When Bob woke up, I said, "I have our answer." The next Sunday we went to the mission church. This time we felt at home and joined.

We served in this mission for four years before we moved away from that city. It was a wonderfully stimulating experience, one that I wouldn't have wanted to miss. As I thrived in the situation, I often wondered why God hadn't answered our prayers earlier. I don't understand why a vigil is sometimes required to receive God's answer. It looks like, if our hearts are sincere, we could just ask God what to do, and He would tell us.

On occasion we may receive His guidance that easily, but other times the process takes time. It's almost as if the process itself is important. Maybe it is. As we pray, we unfold ourselves, opening our will to His leadership. We sift and weigh, changing our perspective to match God's perspective. Our vision widens; our hope rises. We pray on, listening until the moment comes when we have peace and certainty about what choice to make. It's an answer worth praying—and waiting—for, that moment when we know, as Jesus did, "This is the way, walk in it."

making the CONNECTION

What kind of environment for answering do my prayers provide God?

When I'm praying about a choice I have to make, how will I know when God answers?

Notes

1. Hubert Inman Hester, *The Heart of the New Testament* (Nashville: Broadman, 1950, 1963), 142.

2. Ibid., 143.

3. J. W. Shepard, *The Christ of the Gospels: An Exegetical Study* (Grand Rapids: Eerdmans, 1956), 166.

4. Hester, *The Heart of the New Testament,* 143.

5. Elton Trueblood, *The Lord's Prayers* (New York: Harper & Row, 1965), 36.

6. Curtis C. Mitchell, *Praying Jesus' Way* (Old Tappan, N.J.: Revell, 1977), 20.

7. Trueblood, *The Lord's Prayers,* 39.

8. Ibid.

CHAPTER FIVE

WHEN YOU
ARE DISTRACTED

After the people saw the miraculous sign that Jesus did, they began to say, "Surely this is the Prophet who is to come into the world." Jesus, knowing that they intended to come and make him king by force, withdrew again to a mountain by himself. . . .

. . . He went up on a mountainside by himself to pray.

—John 6:14–15; Matthew 14:23

Do you remember the Gospel accounts of Jesus' being tempted in the wilderness? The event occurred right after His baptism. At the end of Luke's account of this incident, there is a line every Christian ought to be familiar with: "When the devil had finished every temptation, he left Him until an opportune time" (Luke 4:13 NASB). The devil is always looking for opportune times to divert us from doing God's will (1 Peter 5:8).

Satan was visibly present and verbally proficient when he tempted Jesus to turn the stones into bread (Matthew 4:3; Luke 4:3). Jesus was fasting when the tempter said, "*If* you are the Son of God, tell these stones to become bread" (Matthew 4:3, italics added). Jesus' hunger naturally made the testing intense, but "deeper still was the tempting to be a bread messiah."[1] In a country where not more than one-fifth of the land was arable under the best of conditions and which was frequently plagued by extremes of drought and flood, bread was a precious commodity.[2] One sure way for Jesus to persuade people to follow Him was to give them bread (John 6:5, 26), but that would have meant bribing men to follow Him. If Jesus were to be God's Messiah, He could not persuade men to follow Him for what they could get out of Him.

At the time, Jesus rejected that way of power. Later, however, the temptation came back, and this time Satan's efforts weren't as obvious. Jesus wasn't alone in the wilderness. He was busy—busy meeting the needs of people.

THE RELENTLESS CROWD

After Jesus chose the twelve apostles, He began training them. He sent them out two by two to minister on their own (Matthew 10:5–42; Mark 6:7–13; Luke 9:1–6). When they returned, they were ready to talk. They wanted to share their experiences. People, though, clamored around them. So many people were coming and going that Jesus and His disciples didn't even have time to eat (Mark 6:31).

Jesus said, "Let's go off to some deserted place where we can get some rest." They got into a boat, perhaps one belonging to one of the apostles, and headed "to a lonely place" (see Mark 6:32 NASB 1977).

Their lonely place, though, didn't turn out to be deserted. People saw them leaving and followed them on foot (Matthew 14:13; Mark 6:33; Luke 9:11). Seeing the boat set sail, the people easily figured out where it was going. They could see the direction it was taking, and they hastened by land around the top of the lake. "At this particular place it was four miles across the lake by boat and ten miles around the top of the lake on foot. On a windless day, or with a contrary wind, a boat might take some time to make the passage, and an energetic person could walk round the top of the lake and be there before the boat arrived."[3] In this case, it was not an energetic person, but an energetic crowd! When Jesus and His men stepped out of the boat, the very crowd from which they had sought relief was waiting. They wanted Him to heal their sick (John 6:2), and they wanted to see His dazzling miracles.

the biggest miracle yet

Jesus had come to find quiet and restful solitude; instead, He found many people intent on getting something from Him. He might have easily resented them and found them to be a nuisance. "What right had they to invade His privacy with their continual demands? Was He to have no rest and quiet and time to Himself at all?"[4] Instead of being annoyed, Jesus' heart was filled with compassion for them (Matthew 14:14). He saw them as "sheep without a shepherd" (Mark 6:34), and He began to teach them (Mark 6:34) and heal their sick (Matthew 14:14).

Late in the afternoon (Luke 9:12), the crowd of more than five thousand people became hungry, and Jesus miraculously provided food for them with five loaves and two fish. This miracle triggered tremendous excitement. So far, they hadn't seen anything like this! "After the people saw the miraculous sign that Jesus did, they began to say, 'Surely this is the Prophet who is to come into the world'" (John 6:14).

The Jews were waiting for the prophet who would be like Moses. Moses had said, "The Lord your God will raise up for you a prophet like me from among you, from your countrymen, you shall listen to him" (Deuteronomy 18:15 NASB). Through Moses, God had miraculously provided bread from heaven (manna Exodus 16:4–36). Now, here was Jesus miraculously providing bread.

The people wanted a leader like Moses—someone to give them free food and political deliverance.[5] They longed for a leader who would drive the Romans from Palestine. They wanted someone who would change the status of Israel from that of a subject nation to that of a world power, who would liberate her from the fate of being an occupied country and exalt her to being the occupier of other nations. They had seen what

Jesus could do, and the thought in their minds was, "This man has power, miraculous and marvelous power. If we can harness Him and His power to our dreams and our plans and our desires, things will begin to happen."[6]

The people were so certain that Jesus would make a terrific king that they were ready to make Him king by force (John 6:15). Jesus quickly perceived what they were planning and took action.

DELIBERATE, PRAYERFUL ACTION

Jesus responded with staccato steps.

- *He sent the disciples away.* The fervor of a crowd is contagious. Jesus did not want the disciples infected with the "Make Jesus King" campaign, for they, too, were thinking of Jesus in terms of earthly power. That would have added to the group's momentum and to the pressure on Him. Jesus made the disciples get into a boat and go on ahead to the other side of the lake (Matthew 14:22).
- *He sent the crowd away.* He calmed the crowd, told them good-bye, and sent them away (Matthew 14:22).
- *He went up into the hills to pray* (see Matthew 14:23). Away from the clamor, the constant movement, the chatter, and the needs of the crowd, Jesus communed with God as He struggled with Satan's latest attempt to derail Him. Subtly and deceptively through needy people, Satan was trying to divert Jesus from the path of suffering and the Cross.

THE KINGDOM WITHOUT THE CROSS

Because Jesus was the Son of God and because He was sinless, it would be easy to conclude that Jesus' staying on the path God had chosen for Him was a simple matter, but it wasn't.

Being sinless meant that He was able to resist temptation (Hebrews 4:15); it didn't mean He was never truly tempted or that He didn't wrestle with it. Never at any time could Jesus have said to Satan, "You know that I can't sin!"

In this instance, His very nature intensified the struggle. With His compassionate heart, He sensed the crowd's strong desire for a Moses-king. He knew they needed a leader because they were "like sheep without a shepherd" (Mark 6:34). The force of their desire tugged at His heartstrings.

- Wouldn't meeting their need for a leader be as compassionate as feeding their physical hunger?
- Couldn't He do a lot of good for the people, even for God, by becoming a political messiah?
- What's wrong with using miraculous power to deliver people from the dominion of the Romans? They are God's people; they deserve to be free.
- What's wrong with reducing hunger and curing ills? God doesn't want people to be hungry or to suffer unnecessarily.

If Jesus were a political king, He could meet the basic needs of the people by political action. He could rid the world of hunger, war, injustice, and poverty without great suffering on His part. As Curtis C. Mitchell wrote, "Here was an opportunity to be king apart from suffering, apart from the cross."[7]

This struggle was so intense that Jesus spent most of the night in prayer. He might have spent more time if the apostles hadn't needed Him. The apostles had set out back across the lake. While they were rowing, a sudden storm came up. Struggling against the winds and the waves, they made little progress. Seeing the boat fighting the waves, Jesus left the hills to help.

How long had Jesus intended to pray? Had He planned on spending the whole night? We don't know, but we do know the time He spent was long enough to align His will with God's will. He returned to the crowd the next day with a "singleness of a heart intent only on God's will and made new in God's power."[8] This is obvious in the courageous and direct way Jesus related to the crowd, who continued to pursue Him.

The crafty, determined crowd caught up with Jesus the next day (John 6:24). Jesus said to them, "I tell you the truth, you are looking for me, not because you saw miraculous signs but because you ate the loaves and had your fill. Do not work for food that spoils, but for food that endures to eternal life, which the Son of Man will give you. On him God the Father has placed his seal of approval" (vv. 26–27).

Jesus revealed Himself as the "bread of life" (vv. 35, 48). This was a real crowd-separator. The people didn't like the idea of spiritual bread; that wasn't what they had in mind. Many decided Jesus' teaching was just too hard (v. 60), and others refused to follow Him any longer (v. 66). Nevertheless, Jesus stayed on track. His praying in the hills enabled Him to resist Satan's temptation, and His example can help us. It provides valuable insight for recognizing and dealing with temptation.

WHEN YOU ARE DISTRACTED

Prayerful solitude is a powerful tool in resisting temptation. It's not the only one,[9] but it is an important one because from time to time we find ourselves in situations like Jesus'.

Satan's opportune time is frequently a complex time in our lives. At this particular time there was many a problem on Jesus' mind and many a burden on His heart. He was under a continuous strain. People were always wanting something from Him. Opposition had formed against Him; the religious leaders were hostile. Realizing His time was limited, He wanted to get His disciples trained. His fellow minister and relative, John the Baptist, had died. Jesus tried to get away to a lonely place by Himself but wasn't successful (Matthew 14:13),[10] so He didn't get the emotional refreshment and spiritual fortification He needed. With various stressful threads winding themselves around Jesus, no wonder the devil saw this as an opportune time to subtly and deceptively to divert Jesus from the path of suffering and the Cross.

When we are busy, when we are weary, when we are burdened down, when we are under stress, Satan sees this as a ripe time for tempting us. The weight of all we are carrying increases our vulnerability. To depart for prayerful solitude is to lessen the weight of what we carry and give God the channel He needs to help us resist temptation.

When Linda was a new missionary in Indonesia, she became very discouraged by the many adjustments she had to make, by friction among some of the missionaries, and by the rejection of many Indonesians to her overtures. This was an opportune time for Satan; he began making her doubt her calling. She was tempted to return home. Finally, in desperation she went to her knees in prayer. She began waking at five in the morning to have uninterrupted time to read the Bible and to pray. God heard and answered Linda's prayers, refreshed her spirit, and renewed her commitment to His call.

The loneliness of some spiritual battles. People surrounded Jesus, but who among them would understand the battle He was experiencing? Who would understand resisting the chance to be king? What would the disciples have advised? If they had prayed with Him, how would they have prayed? Jesus didn't have any human person who would understand. This battle was a lonely one for Jesus.

Seeking the counsel of other believers is an important spiritual tool in fighting many of the temptations we experience, but there are also occasions when the battle will be a lonely one. That is when we find ourselves in a position of decision in which no one understands the conflict. That is when our need for prayerful solitude is especially important. We can wrestle with the temptation without the watchful eyes of others observing us; we can verbalize the struggle without being overheard by someone who may be shocked at what is tempting us. This way our prayer can reach heaven, and God can respond to clarify His will and fortify us to resist temptation.

We may need to take staccato steps to find time to be alone. Like a computer virus, Satan wants to worm his way

61

into our lives and destroy our heart drive. Sometimes his efforts are obvious—what we would label as out-and-out evil. But other times, Satan's efforts aren't as discernible. Even our "good" activities can have distractions lurking in them. When our lives get complicated, as a precautionary measure, it may be a good time to seek solitude to examine our lives and seek God's direction.

Some of Gary's fellow believers began to suspect that the devil was lurking in his complicated life. Gary was the high volume salesman you met in chapter 3. He was becoming more and more obsessed with making money and less and less concerned with customer service. In the early days of his career, his approach had been servantlike: How can I help you? Now it was self-centered: How soon can I close the deal? Sometimes at his weekly Bible study, Gary bragged about some of the manipulative tools he used. Out of concern, Rod, one of the participants, gently suggested Gary needed some time alone with God to evaluate his life. That's when Gary said, "If I take time out, I will only get farther behind."

He added, "The key to my success is quick response to the customer. I always have to be available to answer the phone and to respond to faxes and e-mail messages." He refused to take the steps necessary, such as leaving his home where he worked to find a quiet place with no interruptions where he could realign himself with God's will.

When Rod reminded him that Jesus took time out to pray, Gary responded with, "Yeah, sure, Jesus withdrew; it was easy for Him. He didn't have a schedule to keep, a family to look after, and He lived in a pastoral setting where the population was probably limited."

The pictures we see of Jesus' life certainly give this impression, but Galilee, where He spent the bulk of His ministry, was highly populated. It was a small country, 50 miles from north to south and 25 miles from east to west. Within this small area, there were 204 towns and villages, none with a population of less than 15,000 people.[11] In such a thickly populated area, it was not easy to get away from people for any length of time, as this incident reveals. When He tried to get away after the death of John the Baptist, He couldn't. When He tried again with His disciples, a tenacious crowd was waiting for Him at the retreat site. Finally, He sent the disciples away, sent the crowd away, and went up into the hills to be alone.

Prayer time is not always perfect time. The world isn't put "on hold" so that we can pray. Responsibilities don't end when we close the door to our prayer closet. Even high on the mountain, Jesus was not completely free of other people's needs. From where He was, He could see the disciples out in a boat headed across Lake Galilee to Capernaum. A storm came up. The disciples were frightened. Jesus left the mountain and went to them (John 6:16–21).

When I was a mother of young children, I readily identified with this incident because of the difficulty of finding moments of uninterrupted solitude when no one is going to need you. After our third child was born, my husband agreed to watch our sons every evening after dinner so that I could take a leisurely bath and have some moments for reflection and prayer. So, behind locked doors, I drank in the silence, meditated on Scriptures I had pasted to the wall, and talked with God. Even then, often would come that knock on the door. "Mom, where are my Legos?" "Mom, when are you coming out?" Or, "Brenda, I need your help with the baby."

So I took great reassurance in the fact that while Jesus' time was interrupted, it was still enough time to be fortified. I could leave the bathroom prematurely and go out to help my husband and children, knowing I had given God a channel to work.

Our prayer life isn't always under ideal conditions, but our seeking solitude and doing what we can give God the channel He needs to help us. God will use what we give Him. The God who took the fives loaves and two fish and multiplied them to feed over five thousand people can take what we offer Him and give us what it takes to resist being distracted from doing His will.

makin<u>g</u> the
CONNection

When am I tempted by distractions from doing God's will?

How will withdrawing for prayer help me resist temptation?

Notes

1. William L. Hendricks, *Who Is Jesus Christ? Layman's Library of Christian Doctrine,* vol. 2 (Nashville: Broadman, 1985), 37.

2. *The Interpreter's Bible* (Nashville: Abingdon, 1955), 8:85.

3. William Barclay, *The Gospel of Mark,* 2d ed., The Daily Study Bible (Edinburgh: Saint Andrew, 1956, 1964), 157.

4. William Barclay, *The Gospel of Matthew,* 2d ed., vol. 2, The Daily Study Bible (Edinburgh: Saint Andrew, 1958, 1964), 109.

5. Craig S. Keener, *The IVP Bible Background Commentary New Testament* (Downers Grove, Ill.: InterVarsity, 1993), 279.

6. William Barclay, *The Gospel of John,* 3d ed., vol. 1, The Daily Study Bible (Edinburgh: Saint Andrew, 1964), 209.

7. Curtis C. Mitchell, *Praying Jesus' Way* (Old Tappan, N.J.: Revell, 1977), 22.

8. *The Interpreter's Bible,* 7:433.

9. In the temptation account in Matthew 4:1–11 and Luke 4:1–13, Jesus used Scripture to combat temptation. Other tools for fighting temptation are found in Ephesians 6:11–20.

10. Matthew's account has Jesus going off to a lonely place after hearing about the death of John the Baptist (14:13–14). Mark and Luke have the apostles and Jesus starting out together for a lonely place (Mark 6:30–32; Luke 9:10).

11. Barclay, *The Gospel of Matthew,* 2:109.

am i making
an impact?

Once when Jesus was praying in private and his disciples were with him, he asked them, "Who do the crowds say I am?"

They replied, "Some say John the Baptist; others say Elijah; and still others, that one of the prophets of long ago has come back to life."

"But what about you?" he asked. "Who do you say I am?"

—Luke 9:18–20

Many followers drifted away when they saw that Jesus was not leading them toward a Jewish superstate. Those who traveled with Him hadn't caught on to who He really was even after nearly three years under His teaching (Matthew 16:5–12). The opposition of the Jewish leaders had greatly increased in intensity. An atmosphere of hatred surrounded Jesus. The powerful Pharisees and Sadducees wanted to destroy Him (v. 1). The certainty of the Cross lay ahead.

With time so short, Jesus must have wondered, *Does anyone understand Me? Does anyone recognize who I am?* This was a crucial concern. William Barclay states, "His Kingdom was a kingdom within the hearts of men, and, if there was no one who had enthroned him within his heart, then his Kingdom would have ended before it ever began. But if there was someone who had recognized him and who understood him, even if as yet inadequately, then his work was safe."[1] With His authority, Jesus could have demanded recognition from His followers. He could have repeated who He was over and over until the disciples could spit out the right answer, but that would not have reassured Him. Anyone can memorize facts. Jesus needed something more than that. He needed God's reassurance, so He prayed.

aLONe, BUT NOT aLONe

Jesus withdrew from the crowds to pray, but this time He departed from His usual practice. He took His disciples with Him. He took them north of Galilee to Caesarea Philippi where they could retreat from the crowds. The Bible says, "While He was praying alone, the disciples were with Him" (Luke 9:18 NASB). Why would Jesus, who seemed to value solitude, take the disciples with Him?

- Perhaps Jesus wanted to set an example. He might have wanted them to connect His determination and strength with prayer. It would be sometime after this when they would ask, "Lord, teach us to pray" (Luke 11:1).

- Perhaps Jesus wanted the disciples there as a buffer. Their presence might have served as protection from the constant demands of the people. In the last chapter, we saw how the crowd doggedly pursued Him when He sought solitude. Shortly after this, He attempted to retreat with His apostles to the area around Tyre and Sidon. Here, where the mountains came down almost to the sea, He could have a cool, restful retreat, but even here, His fame had spread. "He entered a house and did not want anyone to know it; yet he could not keep his presence secret" (Mark 7:24).

- There's also the possibility that Jesus wanted the comfort of their companionship. One of the reasons He chose them was "that they might be with him" (Mark 3:14). Although solitude is preferable for praying about many of our spiritual struggles, there will be times when we want the presence of others. They can be engaging in prayer with us, and even if they aren't, their nearness can be comforting and supportive.

- Or perhaps the disciples were present because it was to them that He was looking for the reassurance He needed. After all, these were the ones who had been with Him day in, day out. They had heard His bold, startling teaching, watched Him heal, and watched Him make decisions. Had they discovered yet who He really was?

the all-important questions

After Jesus prayed, He began asking the disciples questions. First, He asked, "Who do the crowds say I am?" (Luke 9:18). Having mixed with the multitude, the disciples were aware of the various opinions about Jesus. Several answers were given.

"John the Baptist." Here the disciples were probably quoting the ruler Herod Antipas's terrified opinion. He was scared that Jesus was a ghost sent to haunt him for murdering John the Baptist.

"Elijah." Elijah had been taken up without dying, and Malachi said Elijah would return again. It's not stated specifically, but Jeremiah may also have been mentioned, for some Jews believed that before the Messiah came, Jeremiah would return and reveal where the ark of the covenant and the altar of incense from Solomon's temple were.

"One of the prophets." This was a compliment. If the people regarded Jesus as a prophet, they regarded Him as a man within the confidence of God (Amos 3:7).

Actually, all of the answers were intended to be compliments, but that was not what Jesus wanted or needed. Jesus pressed for a deeper answer. To those who had been with Him day by day, He asked, "What about you? Who do you say I am?" (v. 20).

Simon Peter answered, "You are the Christ, the Son of the living God" (Matthew 16:16).

THE REASSURING ANSWER

Jesus exulted in Peter's answer that He was the Christ, the Messiah, the Anointed One. Peter recognized who He was! Here was His reassurance. He said, "Blessed are you, Simon son of Jonah, for this was not revealed to you by man, but by my Father in heaven" (Matthew 16:17).

In His exultation, Jesus made promises to Peter:

- "I will build my church" on you (v. 18).
- "I will give you the keys of the kingdom of heaven" (v. 19).
- "Whatever you bind on earth will be bound in heaven, and whatever you loose on earth will be loosed in heaven" (v. 19).

Jesus took His disciples apart for the all-important purpose of finding out if there was anyone who recognized Him. "To his joy one man did understand, and Jesus was committing his work into the hands of that man."[2]

As joyful as Jesus was, He asked them not to tell anyone He was the Messiah (v. 20). The reassurance was for His sake; it was not an announcement to be shared with the world at this time.

WHEN WE NEED REASSURANCE

From time to time in the Christian life, we may find ourselves in need of reassurance. We worship an invisible God who whispers to us in a still, small voice, so we may wonder at times, *Am I hearing correctly?* Sometimes we may wonder if this path of faith we are walking is leading anywhere. At other times we may have thought we were leading others to grasp God's vision, and yet no one seems to catch our excitement. We wonder, *Am I seeing correctly? If I am, shouldn't someone be catching on?* Occasionally, we think we perceive God's plan for our future, but it is so scary that we dare not take another step without some reassurance.

Jesus' prayer at Caesarea Philippi doesn't tell us everything we need to know about seeking reassurance, but it offers some helpful insights.

God doesn't always answer directly. God answers prayers in a variety of ways. Often it is the "This is the way, walk ye in it" type of reassurance—an inner witness of the Holy Spirit—the type of answer God gave Jesus when He made a choice about who the apostles would be. Sometimes God answers by giving us tools that will lead us to the answer. When Jesus prayed for reassurance, God responded by giving Him a tool—questions to ask. When Jesus used those questions, God gave Him the reassurance He needed.

When John (not the same John mentioned in chapter 3) needed reassurance, God nudged him to talk to someone.

The spring and summer before John went to college,[3] he experienced a spiritual growth spurt. He earnestly and conscientiously sought God's will. As he led his church's youth group, the older members marveled at his maturity. He seemed so strong and sure of himself.

John took his Christian zeal with him to a large state university. Noticing the extensive immorality on campus, John organized a Bible study in his dorm. He was surprised by how much preparation time was required, and college itself was far more demanding than he had thought it would be. Neither had he counted on spending so much time in the lab. After three months, his Bible study dwindled to two others and himself. John felt like he was "running on empty."

John was haunted by his need to know if he was correctly living the Christian life. Urgently and passionately, he prayed about it. One morning on the way to the cafeteria, the thought came to him that he ought to talk with Dr. Miller, his major professor and one of the few Christian faculty members on campus.

When John told Dr. Miller about his concern, Dr. Miller responded, "John, I've noticed your struggle to try to keep up with your studies, your lab hours, and also prepare for the Bible studies. You are trying to do too much. I advise you to concentrate on your studies so that you can be a well-trained person to lead Bible studies *after* college. This doesn't mean you should let up in your moral stand or in your devotional life, but do give up the Bible study. You are not a strong enough student to handle it all."

With a clarity John hadn't had before, he saw his personal limitations. A peace welled up in his heart as he recognized God's answer in Dr. Miller's words. He now knew what to do and was reassured about how to live the Christian life.

Jesus' praying in the presence of others shows that we do not always have to be alone to pray effectively. Jesus' retreating for prayer with His disciples does not negate the emphasis we've been giving to solitude. What we are beginning to see—and will continue to see—is some variety in Jesus' prayer life, and there should be in ours as well. Otherwise, our prayer life can become a series of rote exercises instead of dynamic interactions with a living God. Plus there are times when praying with others can add a supernatural dimension that can be very reassuring.

For several years I prayed once a month with June and Susan. We took turns meeting in each other's homes. Our children were either out on their own or in school, so our homes were quiet. Each time we gathered was like a mini retreat. I remember one occasion being concerned about my future, believing I was discerning God's call but needing reassurance because appropriate doors weren't opening. Was I hearing Him correctly? I shared my puzzlement with June and Susan, and as we prayed aloud together, June asked that God speak to me through Bob, my husband.

Actually, I should have thought of that. Whatever my future path took, it would involve my husband. Perhaps I should have been discussing this with him, but I hadn't. I said to myself, *I will talk to Bob about this sometime,* but before I got around to it, Bob spoke to me about the direction he saw my future going. What he saw was right in line with what I was perceiving God's call to be. How reassuring Bob's words were! Joy bubbled up within me, for I realized that flesh and blood didn't reveal this, but our Father in heaven did.

God's answer may not be perfect in the sense that we will no longer have any struggles. When Jesus chose the Twelve (see chapter 4), God's answer was not perfect. One of them eventually denied Jesus, and another one betrayed Him to His enemies.

At Caesarea Philippi, Jesus was joyful that Peter recognized Him as the Christ, the Messiah, even though Peter and the other disciples did not fully comprehend what it meant. When Jesus tried to explain, Peter rebuked Him (Matthew 16:22). Jesus connected being the Messiah with suffering and death. To the disciples His statements were both incredible and incomprehensible. All their lives they had thought of the Messiah in terms of irresistible conquest; now Jesus presented ideas that staggered them. Advanced as Peter's insight was, he rejected the idea of a suffering Messiah (v. 22). Jesus still had work to do.

God's answer will be sufficient. God didn't always answer Jesus directly, nor did He always give Him perfect answers, but He gave Him sufficient answers. The men Jesus chose to be His apostles changed the world. Peter's answer gave Jesus the reassurance He needed. His close followers were beginning to perceive who He really was; He had ignited a torch in their hearts that would never go out. Although the flame might have been very small at that time, it was strong enough to serve as a springboard for Jesus to teach His disciples the truth about the future.

God's answer may not be specifically what we have asked for, but it will be sufficient to meet our needs. God always answers a person. This insight helped me to understand a conversation I had with a group of older friends—women whom I had met earlier in my life when my children were small. We were in a prayer group together. With their own children grown, they were a valuable source of advice and encouragement. Later, after I moved away, I would see May, Ramona, Georgia, and Geneva at various denominational meetings.

On one such occasion I came to a meeting rather cynical about the Christian life. My analysis skills that help me as a writer and a biblical interpreter also make it easy to be cynical. In fighting it, I've learned I am particularly susceptible when I'm discouraged, as I was this particular time we met.

May, Ramona, Georgia, and I were talking when Geneva joined us.

As she approached, I noticed her right hand was sticking out of her blouse as if she were holding her arm close to her body. Geneva's left-hand had previously been crippled from surgery that had not gone well. Smiling from ear to ear, Geneva greeted us with, "I tell you, girls, God can do anything!"

Well, not everything, I thought. I didn't say that out loud because Geneva was glowing. Instead, I said, "Have you had something unusual happen to you, Geneva?"

Geneva, age seventy-eight, told us how she had gone for a walk a few weeks earlier. It had been raining, and she walked along a street where there was no curbing or sidewalk. She decided to run so that she could get back in time to watch the evening news.

"Run?" I asked.

"Oh, yeah, I can run like a blue racer snake. As I started running, a car came along, and I moved over onto the grass to get out of the way. That's when I slipped on the wet grass and slid down into the ditch. I tried to get up, but I couldn't use either arm. The pain in my right shoulder and my limp arm told me I had broken my shoulder. Of course, I can't do anything with my left hand. Whatever progress I made with my feet was soon canceled because I would slide on the wet grass back down into the ditch. No one could see me sitting in the ditch because it was about three-and-a-half-feet deep. No one could hear me yelling for help. I wondered if I would be spending the night in the ditch.

"Finally, desperate, I looked up to heaven and prayed, 'God, I know this is my fault. I shouldn't have tried to run. I'm sorry.

Won't You please help me get out of here?'

"After I prayed, something lifted my body up and kept me going. I walked out of the ditch and walked three blocks home. Actually, it was like I floated all the way home. I tell you, girls, we don't have to worry; whatever we need God is going to provide."

I waited for "the girls" to say something like, "Well, not every time," or, "He can't do *everything.*" Georgia was eighty-six, Ramona ninety-three, and May ninety-three. They had lived long, and their lives hadn't been easy. Among them, they had experienced the death of spouses, heart problems, paralysis, burns, illnesses, moves, heartaches, and disappointments. From the way I saw it, many times God hadn't come through.

What "the girls" said, though, were comments such as, "Yes, Georgia, that's right," "He sure will," and "I'll amen that."

I looked at their faces, checking for traces of the cynicism that was in my heart, and I saw that they were sincere. In that moment, their faith jump-started mine, and the cloud of discouragement hanging over my head dissipated.

I didn't, though, have an explanation for their confidence in God until I studied this incident in Jesus' prayer life. As I saw how God always answered Jesus, I realized He had always answered these women. He didn't give them perfect answers, but He gave them sufficient answers to meet the heartaches of life. No wonder their confidence in Him was so strong.

As we have seen and will continue to see, Jesus brought His needs to God through prayer. God always responded by giving Him what He needed to carry on. God's answers did not always mean the end of struggle, but they were sufficient. *God always answered Jesus,* and that's what we can count on when we pray. God will always answer us.

making the
CONNECTION

What is the difference between a perfect answer and a sufficient answer?

What is one dimension that praying with others can bring to my prayer life?

Notes

1. William Barclay, *The Mind of Jesus* (New York: Harper & Row, 1960, 1961), 167.
2. Ibid.
3. John's story was told in my book *Not My Will But Thine* (Nashville: Broadman & Holman, 1998).

WHEN YOU ARE DISCOURAGED

And He was saying to them all, "If anyone wishes to come after Me, let him deny himself, and take up his cross daily and follow Me. For whoever wishes to save his life will lose it, but whoever loses his life for My sake, he is the one who will save it. For what is a man profited if he gains the whole world, and loses or forfeits himself?" . . .

Some eight days after these sayings, He took along Peter and John and James, and went up on the mountain to pray.

— Luke 9:23–25, 28 NASB

Peter's confession of "You are the Christ" (Matthew 16:16) must have been an important signal to Jesus in His training of the apostles, for the Bible says, "From that time on Jesus began to explain" what was ahead (v. 21). He began revealing in plain, matter-of-fact statements. First, He told them that He had to go to Jerusalem (v. 21). Second, He told them that He had to suffer many things at the hands of the elders, chief priests, and teachers of the law (v. 21; also Mark 8:31; Luke 9:22). Third, He told them the plain, rude, shocking fact of His death. He had to be killed. (Jesus still hadn't mentioned the Cross. The fact of His death had to be revealed first.) Finally, Jesus attempted to relieve the dark message of death by the bright hope of the Resurrection. He would be raised up on the third day, but the disciples did not catch that hope.

His disciples must have been too shocked by Jesus' words about death and enemies to hear the words of hope. A suffering Messiah was entirely foreign to their way of thinking. The Messiah was to be a conqueror, not One to die at the hands of His enemies.

Surely, they thought, *He has taken too gloomy a view of the united opposition of the Pharisees and Sadducees.* Bold, impetuous Peter took Jesus aside and spoke what they all must have been thinking. Peter, who had just received approval from Jesus for his recognition of who He was, rebuked Jesus: "God forbid it, Lord! This shall never happen to You" (Matthew 16:22 NASB).

Now Jesus must have been the one surprised, because He turned around and addressed Peter sternly. "Get behind Me, Satan! You are a stumbling block to Me; for you are not settling your mind on God's interests, but man's" (v. 23 NASB).

Why did Jesus issue this stinging rebuke?

- Perhaps Jesus was grieved that Peter—the one who had made such a noble confession of faith—didn't have a fuller grasp of what being the Messiah meant. Many teachers have moments of discouragement when they wonder, *Aren't my students ever going to catch on?* All through Jesus' ministry there had been half-veiled intimations about the necessity of His dying (Matthew 9:15; 16:4; John 2:19; 3:14; 6:51), but none of those symbolic references had been fully understood by the twelve apostles.

- Since Jesus called Peter "Satan," He may have seen Peter's concern as tempting Him to get off course the way Satan had tried to tempt Him in the wilderness. This time, though, the temptation came from one Jesus loved and praised. That made it harder to resist, which may be why He responded so swiftly and decisively.

- When Jesus spoke the words out loud about His suffering and death, perhaps He was reminded of the reality of what was ahead (implied in Luke 9:31). By His strong answer, perhaps Jesus was saying, "This is awful enough as it is, Peter. Don't tempt Me by suggesting there is a way out."

Jesus didn't try to soften His retort; instead, He proceeded in Matthew 16 to teach what following Him really meant:

- Deny yourself (v. 24).
- Take up your cross (v. 24).
- Lose your life to save it (v. 25).
- Forfeit the world's gain (v. 26).

You can almost hear His listeners gasp, "This teaching is too hard." Peter must have thought of the words he said on another occasion, "We have left everything to follow you!" (Matthew 19:27).

Trying to teach the disciples what the Messiah was like and what true followship meant must have been discouraging for Jesus. Discouragement can make us question what we are doing, and Jesus needed to be certain He had understood God correctly as He headed for Jerusalem. About a week after He began His hard, clear teaching, Jesus withdrew to a mountaintop to pray, and He took Peter, James, and John with Him (Luke 9:28).

the ministry of prayer

Why did Jesus take Peter, James, and John with Him? I think I would have been tempted to leave Peter behind with the other members of the Twelve!

It could have been the protection factor we mentioned in the last chapter. They provided a shield against interruptions.

It could have been the comfort factor. At this time of discouragement, Jesus needed the presence of those committed to working and traveling with Him.

It could have been that Jesus' taking them to the mountaintop reflected His desire to meet their needs as well as His own. If they were recoiling against what He told them, then perhaps prayer would encourage them too.

Now Jesus could have prayed for them without their being present, but there is a ministry of prayer when we pray for others in their presence. Think about the difference it makes to you when someone says, "I'll pray for you," and when someone says, "Let me pray for you, right now, right here."

Although we can see all kinds of possibilities for Jesus' taking Peter, James, and John with Him, I don't think the three anticipated much. Weary after the day's activities and the ascent of the mountain, they soon fell asleep. While they slept, Jesus prayed, and His prayer reached heaven.

GOD'S TRANSFORMING ANSWER

While Jesus was praying, His countenance was altered (Luke 9:29). His garments "became white and gleaming" (Luke 9:29 NASB), literally meaning flashing like lightning.

Roused by the splendor, the disciples woke up. When they were wide awake, they saw Jesus' glory. They also saw Moses and Elijah talking with Jesus. This sparked a conversation between Peter and Jesus. While they were talking, a cloud appeared and covered them with its shadow. God's voice from the cloud said, "This is my Son, whom I have chosen; listen to him" (v. 35 NIV).

This event gives us a graphic picture of how God encouraged Jesus. "Every line of the picture portrays God's visitation."[1]

The change in countenance. As Jesus prayed, an inner change took place. The first outward evidence that God was renewing Jesus' strength was a change in His countenance. "His face shone like the sun" (Matthew 17:2).

The change in raiment. "There was a kind of effulgence— a celestial radiance—shining out over all. The Divinity within broke through the veil of the flesh and shone out, until His very raiment kindled to the dazzling brightness of the light."[2]

The appearance of Moses and Elijah. Here were two supreme figures among the Jews: Moses was the supreme law-giver, and Elijah was the supreme prophet. Their appearance encouraged Jesus. "It is as if they said to him: 'It is you who are right, and it is the popular teachers who are wrong; it is you in whom there is the fulfillment of all that the law says and all that the prophets foretold. The real fulfillment of the past is not in the popular idea of might and power, but in your way of sacrificial love.'"[3]

Moses and Elijah's conversation with Jesus. They spoke about the way Jesus would fulfill God's purpose by dying in Jerusalem (Luke 9:31). "What two better people to talk to Jesus about dying than Moses and Elijah? They were representative of those who witnessed and suffered for God and for whom the end was not tragedy but triumph. The encouragement for Jesus was that if he went on, there would certainly be a cross, but there would equally certainly be the glory."[4]

The cloud that appeared. The cloud is thought to be the Shechinah glory of God. All through the history of Israel there was the idea of the Shechinah, the glory of God. Again and again this glory appeared to the people in the form of a cloud. Now the glory of God was upon Jesus, assuring Him of God's approval of what He was doing.

God's audible words. In the Greek, God's words go something like this: "This is My Son, the dearly-beloved one; be constantly hearing Him" (v. 35). God was confirming the rightness of Jesus' interpretation of Himself and of what it means to follow Him.

"For Jesus the transfiguration brought new strength . . . and added patience, through a foretaste of the glory He should experience after His passion."[5]

ENCOURAGEMENT FOR THE DISCIPLES

When Peter, James, and John saw Jesus' shining face and His glistening garments, they were "eyewitnesses of his majesty"

(2 Peter 1:16). No Jew would have seen that luminous cloud without thinking of the glory of God resting upon His people. Here was something that would lift up the hearts of the disciples. Here was something that would enable them to see the glory beyond the shame and humiliation.

When the disciples heard God's voice, they fell on their faces in awe and were afraid. Ray Summers, in his *Commentary on Luke,* describes the significance of this event:

> *This is my Son* indicates that the voice spoke to the three disciples and for their benefit. In the baptism experience the same phrase had been used (from Psalm 2:7), but it was directed to Jesus. . . . At the baptism, the voice said to Jesus, "You are my Son"; at the transfiguration it said to the disciples, "This is my Son."
>
> *Listen to him:* The tense of the imperative indicates continuous action—"keep on listening to him." The chain of events starting with Peter's confession indicates that the command to listen referred to their listening to what Jesus was saying about his death. They had confessed faith that Jesus was the Son of God, and now the voice from heaven—right out of the cloud of God's presence—confirmed that confession. . . . The voice from heaven was saying essentially, "Keep on listening to what he is saying about the necessity of his death."[6]

Peter, James, and John still did not fully understand (as future events would reveal), but the Transfiguration gave them some glimmering hope that the future was not all grim.

God's encouragement to Jesus, Peter, James, and John in response to Jesus' praying should encourage us to pray when we are discouraged.

NEEDED: A GLIMPSE OF GLORY

One of the psalmists said, "I would have despaired unless I had believed that I would see the goodness of the Lord in the land of the living" (Psalm 27:13 NASB). Serving God and doing

His will can sometimes become so hard that, like the psalmist, we would despair if we couldn't see evidence of God at work.

My friend, Janice, directs a ministry called HOPE (Helping Others Pursue Excellence) in which she dispenses food, clothing, housing, and advice to needy individuals. She said:

> I'm a person who likes to get things shaped up, organized, and moving. I like to see tangible results and success, but I have always been drawn to serving in areas where quick results and success stories are not the norm. Galatians 6:9 says, "Let us not lose heart in doing good, for in due time we shall reap if we do not grow weary" (NASB). Here's my paraphrase of that: "There's lots to do, you'll get tired; keep doing it anyway, don't give up." But what is there to sustain me along the way? When the prayers are prayed, the lessons are taught, the food handed out, the effort made, and the burden of keeping on keeping on weighs almost too heavy to bear, then what? God gives me a glimpse of glory. He allows me to be a part of leading a child to Christ, to understand that success is not measured in matters of attendance or offering or facilities, but in changed lives which occasionally I get to witness.[7]

A glimpse of glory helps her to carry on.

The psalmist's advice was to "wait on the Lord" (Psalm 27:14 KJV). In the Old Testament, this phrase frequently refers to prayer. In other words, pray to the Lord so that your heart will take courage and you will be strengthened, which is what Jesus did when He took Peter, James, and John with Him to a mountaintop to pray.

So when the going gets rough . . .

- when you have confronted too many barriers too close together,
- when your burdens become too heavy,
- when you have to face things that are almost unbearable to bear,

- when you have witnessed and witnessed and no one responds to the gospel,
- when you have served and served without seeing any visible results,
- when you have lost your enthusiasm for serving the Lord, or
- when you have concluded that it is simply not worth trying any more,

  it is time to withdraw and ask God for a glimpse of glory.

Though the Holy Spirit is given to us as a pledge of all God will ultimately bestow on us (2 Corintians 1:22; 5:5; Ephesians 1:13–14), we still sometimes need a partial glimpse, some transfiguration experience here on earth, to enable us to carry on.

Through prayer we can be spiritually transformed. This is when "we are most likely to witness, in whatever measure may be possible for us, the glory of God."[8] We can be changed and renewed. When we ask for a glimpse of glory, God will answer appropriately, giving us what we need to carry on.

JUST A SMALL GLIMPSE WILL DO.

Our glimpse of glory doesn't have to be spectacular such as Jesus' transfiguration. A small rift in the sky to let God's glory shine through may be just enough to keep us from giving up. It is for me. I remember one fall when I was teaching Bible literature to college students. I had no energy or interest in beginning another semester. I never thought I would feel that way because I love teaching the Bible, but there's a lot of stress involved in teaching unmotivated students. Its cumulative effect caught up with me, and I loathed the thought of beginning another semester. Trying to interest students in a subject they were required to take did not make for a warm environment for studying God's Word.

The first class session, as I looked at their disinterested faces propped on elbows with their faces on the clock, I spit out the words like a tape recorder. As I left the class the second night, I thought, *I can't go on like this the whole semester.* That week I prayed for a renewing of my spirit, some glimpse of God's glory that would enable me to go on.

The third evening session had already started when a woman in her late thirties entered the classroom. As Darlene placed her late admittance slip on the lectern, I thought, *Oh, boy, here's another disinterested student, joining us late, adding to the lacklusterness of this class.* But an hour or so into the class, Darlene began asking questions. I perked up. Here was an interested student. The other students began to sit up and show more interest. It was almost as if her attentiveness was saying to them, "It's all right. You can be interested in the Bible without being uncool."

After several class sessions, Darlene lingered after class one night, and we talked. That's when she told me about her terminal disease. She said, "I want to get my life in order before I die and make provisions for my children. I want to teach them about God. That's why I hold on to every word you say. Whatever you teach me here, I go home and teach my children."

Talk about a transfiguration experience! I suddenly had a renewed vision of what a glorious opportunity it was to teach the Bible. I'm sure the change was visible in my countenance immediately as I realized God had given me a beachhead for sharing the gospel. You never know what needs are present among the individuals in a classroom.

Interestingly, Darlene didn't complete the class. She couldn't handle the class requirements, her illness, the needs of her children, strife with her ex-husbands, and her meager finances, but I taught on with vigor and enthusiasm after she left because God had sent her. Through her, He had given me a glimpse of glory.

when the glimpse is spectacular

Occasionally, God's encouragement in response to our praying may be spectacular, *at least to us.* The nature of the experience may be so unusual or dramatic that we may be tempted to magnify it as Peter did. He wanted to prepare three shelters and linger on the mountain (Matthew 17:4; Mark 9:5; Luke 9:33). He wanted to prolong the great moment and not return to the everyday world. Likewise, we may want to focus on God's encouragement so much that we lose sight of why God gave it to us.

Or, the relief we experience—whether the glimpse of glory is small or spectacular—may be misleading. We may assume that our struggle is over when it isn't. Experiencing the glory of God did not prompt Jesus to remain on the mountain. It put Him right back on the path He had been walking—the path toward the cross.

Our glimpse of glory is to be a temporary support. It is to give us strength to keep walking. As the Bible says, "Those who *wait for the Lord* will gain new strength; they will mount up with wings like eagles, they will run and not get tired, they will walk and not become weary" (Isaiah 40:31 NASB, italics added).

making the
CONNeCtiON

Is spiritual transfiguration something that could happen only to Jesus?

How may I seek a glimpse of glory?

Notes

1. *The Interpreter's Bible* (Nashville: Abingdon, 1955), 7:458.

2. J. W. Shepard, *The Christ of the Gospels: An Exegetical Study* (Grand Rapids: Eerdmans, 1956), 315.

3. William Barclay, *The Mind of Jesus* (New York: Harper & Row, 1960, 1961), 180–81.

4. Ibid., 181.

5. Shepard, *Christ of the Gospels,* 317.

6. Ray Summers, *Commentary on Luke* (Waco, Tex.: Word, 1972), 116.

7. E-mail message from Janice Post, December 6, 2000.

8. *The Interpreter's Bible,* 8:174.

PART TWO

thanksgiving

ReCOGNIZING the ULtimate SOURCe

When he was at the table with them, he took bread, gave thanks, broke it and began to give it to them. Then their eyes were opened.
—Luke 24:30-31

John, the father of four that you met in chapter 3, will probably always associate his mother's prayer life with hair dryers. John said, "Each morning as I was getting ready for school, my mother would be under the hair dryer, Bible in hand, reading and praying. At the time, I kind of sloughed it off, something silly that mothers do, but now it is a sacred memory, spurring me on to be faithful in praying for my own children."

What would your friends or family members associate with your praying? Callused knees? Eloquent words? Your conversational style? A certain tone of voice?

Some of Jesus' disciples associated His prayer life with praying hands and a grateful heart. In fact, it was this association that helped them solve a mystery.

WHO IS HE?

When the resurrected Jesus appeared to two of the disciples as they were returning home to Emmaus, they didn't recognize Him. The last person they expected to see was Jesus! After all, they had been in Jerusalem; they had witnessed the Crucifixion. Jesus was dead. That was a fact.

The "stranger" said to them, "What are you talking about as you walk along?"[1]

Looking gloomy, one of them asked, "Are You the only person who doesn't know the things that have been happening in Jerusalem?"

Jesus asked, "What sort of things?"

"The things that happened to Jesus of Nazareth," they answered. "He was a prophet, mighty in what He said and did. Our leaders handed Him over to be sentenced to death, and He was crucified. And we had hoped that He would be the one who was going to set Israel free! Besides all that, this is now the third day since it happened. Some of the women of our group surprised us; they went at dawn to the tomb, but could not find His body. They came back saying they had seen a vision of angels who told them that He is alive. Some of our group went to the tomb and found it exactly as the women had said, but they did not see Him."

Jesus chided them a bit. "How foolish you are, how slow you are to believe what the prophets said!" Then He went on to explain to them what the Scriptures had said about Him. Still the disciples did not recognize Him.

As they approached Emmaus, Jesus acted as if He were going on, but they urged Him to stay, and so He did. "When he was at the table with them, he took bread, gave thanks, broke it and began to give it to them. Then their eyes were opened and they recognized him" (Luke 24:30–31). Jesus was alive!

This was too good to keep to themselves, so they hurriedly returned to Jerusalem. They told the other disciples how they recognized Jesus when He broke the bread as He blessed it (v. 35). This was something they all had seen Him do many times. They could recall lunches when Jesus broke off hunks of bread for each of them. There were evening campfires when they dipped pieces of bread in broth.

There were numerous commonplace occasions like these when Jesus thanked God, but there were also some unusual times, too, when Jesus' hands—and heart—expressed thanksgiving. Let's look at those.

PRAYING HANDS at WORK

The feeding of the five thousand. In chapter 5, we saw how the people who followed Jesus across the lake lingered and listened to Him throughout the afternoon. As hunger set in, the disciples wanted to send the people away so they could go to the nearby farms and villages to buy food (Matthew 14:15; Mark 6:36), but Jesus chose to feed them. He looked around at the available resources, which were five loaves and two fish. Holding them in His hands, He looked up to heaven and thanked God, and the loaves and the fish became more than enough to feed the crowd of over five thousand.[2]

The feeding of the four thousand. Sometime after the feeding of the five thousand, another crowd gathered and stayed with Him for three days. Jesus became concerned about their hunger. Among them they had seven loaves. Jesus took the loaves in His hands and gave thanks to God (Mark 8:6). They also had a few small fish (v. 7), and Jesus gave thanks for those also. Over four thousand people ate and were filled.[3]

The blessing of children. As the crowds continued to follow Jesus, the opposition grew more open. The Pharisees tried to trap Him by asking difficult questions. After dealing with a particularly tricky question (Mark 10:2), Jesus and His disciples went into a house, where they continued talking. It was probably the kind of stimulating conversation where the last thing you wanted was an interruption, so the disciples weren't too pleased when parents knocked on the door. They asked,

"Would Jesus please bless our children?"

When Jesus noticed the displeasure of the disciples, He immediately beckoned the parents and children to come in. At the same time, He admonished the disciples for their thoughtlessness.

> He said to them, "Let the little children come to me, and do not hinder them, for the kingdom of God belongs to such as these. I tell you the truth, anyone who will not receive the kingdom of God like a little child will never enter it." And he took the children in his arms, put his hands on them and blessed them. (Mark 10:14–16)[4]

Blessing the bread and the wine. Shortly before His death, Jesus participated in the traditional Passover meal with His disciples. Together they ate the traditional roasted lamb, unleavened bread, wine, and bitter herbs. When the time came for explaining the symbolism of this ancient feast, Jesus departed from tradition. He took a piece of bread in His hand and said a prayer of thanks. He broke the bread, gave it to the disciples, and told them, "'This is my body.' Then he took the cup [of wine], gave thanks and offered it to them, saying, 'Drink from it, all of you. This is my blood of the covenant, which is poured out for many for the forgiveness of sins'" (Matthew 26:27).

Hands breaking bread and giving thanks.

Hands cradling children and blessing them.

Hands holding a cup of wine and expressing gratitude.

No wonder the Emmaus disciples recognized the resurrected Jesus by an act of thanksgiving. Thanksgiving was an integral part of Jesus' prayer life, as these instances and the ones in the next two chapters show. That's why we are calling it the second cornerstone. After solitude, thanksgiving was the most prominent feature of Jesus' prayer life. The question is, Shall we make thanksgiving a prominent part of ours?

I raise the question for two reasons.

WHY WE ask

We may not be as motivated to try thanksgiving as we are the other cornerstones of Jesus' prayer life. If we are facing a crisis, making a tough choice, or feeling pressed, there's an urgency present that motivates us to pray. We seek times of solitude and honestly express how we feel to find solutions to our dilemmas. We're interested in intercession because we all pray for others at some time or other, usually when they are in a crisis situation. But giving thanks implies that something has already happened; the crisis is past, hence, the lack of urgency.

Jesus' thanks seem commonplace and routine as if they have no real bearing on the events themselves. Isn't giving thanks—whether it is with two, twelve, or five thousand—like saying, "God is great, God is good, let us thank Him for our food?" All good Jews thanked God for their food. They also asked rabbis and rulers of synagogues to bless their children. Wasn't Jesus just performing expected rituals?

Consequently, we may be tempted to dismiss Jesus' thanks as nice but not applicable, as if they offer no insight for strengthening our prayer life. Maybe we need a second look.

ONe moRe Look

It's true. Jesus didn't have to say thanks in order to multiply the loaves and the fish to feed the large crowds. Most of His miracles were performed without praying, let alone a prayer of thanks.

Neither did Jesus have to say thanks when introducing the symbolic elements of the new covenant. Prayers associated with the Passover meal had already been said. If He were just doing what was routine, those prayers would have been enough.

Jesus didn't have to take the children in His arms to bless them. All the parents expected was a perfunctory touch and prayer. "When Jesus embraced those children, he expressed affection for them. He did not make his prayer an alien ritual-istic formal affair but a natural, intimate aspect of life."[5]

Rather, Jesus paused and thanked the Father because He wanted to acknowledge God as the Source.

- When He took the loaves and the fish in His hands, looked up to heaven, and gave thanks, He recognized God as the One who gives us bread, who gives us life, and who provides for our needs.

- When He held the children and blessed them, He credited God with creating life and acknowledged Him as the One who can make our lives full and happy.

- When He thanked God for the bread and the wine, attaching meaning to each, He recognized God's efforts to reconcile us to Him. A new covenant was being initiated, and His prayer of thanks connected it to the Father.

- In praying the night before His death, Jesus gratefully referred to disciples as "those whom you gave me" (John 17:6).

- When He went home with the Emmaus disciples and broke bread with them, even after all that had happened, He continued His practice of relating everything to God and did so right up to His final earthly prayer. As He ascended into heaven (Luke 24:50–51), He blessed the disciples. He lifted up His hands—a gesture that gratefully acknowledged God as the one who had given them to Him.

Jesus took nothing for granted. He expressed gratitude because He humbly recognized that everything comes from somewhere else. People, objects, and events are here because God the Father wants them here. With praying hands and a grateful heart, Jesus connected them with their Ultimate Source, and I recommend doing the same. It will enrich your prayer life.

WHAT GIVING THANKS ADDS

If we relate every person, object, and event to its Ultimate Source, we will have a heightened sense of God's presence and power.

Heightened sense of God's presence. In a nebulous way, we all know God is ever present, but a conscious awareness of this sometimes eludes us for any number of reasons.

- We may be so busy and preoccupied with the matters of life that our sense of wonder—that childlike quality which readily perceives God—becomes eroded.
- We get in a rut and take life and Him for granted.
- Life's hard knocks leave us cynical. We begin to think of the world as a hostile place where God is just barely present and His power limited.
- Our anxieties and fears may overpower our God awareness.
- In the pursuit to get ahead, our focus may be so keen that we become blind and insensitive to the goodness and mercy of God.

Relating every person, thing, and event to God takes off the blinders, and our senses become alive to His presence, His blessings, and His activity in the world. The world becomes a less hostile place, we feel closer to God, and praying becomes easier. We have the sense that God is near and ready to listen, which makes us eager to talk.

Heightened sense of God's power. As we become more aware of God's presence, His blessings, and His activity, our faith increases. A sense of expectancy develops. Our outlook improves. Anything becomes possible in the same world with God. That's why Jesus could take in His hands a few loaves of bread and some fish and expect the Father to multiply the amount to feed thousands. He didn't petition God to do it; rather, He gave thanks, knowing that God would provide (more about this in the next chapter). Because He related everything to its Ultimate Source, Jesus believed that anything was possible with God.

We can increase our awareness of God and His power by relating every thing and every experience to its Ultimate Source. How do we do this? The same way Jesus did—by giving thanks.

DEVELOPING a GRATEFUL HEART LIKE JESUS'

Recently someone gave me a book about being grateful. It begins this way: "A grateful heart is a gift from God. Left to our own initiative, we might never develop one." I disagree. I believe it takes initiative to develop a grateful heart, and here are some ways we can do that.

Begin your prayers with thanksgiving. Before any petition is voiced, thank God for something whether you *feel* grateful or not. Feel free to begin with generic items, such as, "Thank You for a good night's rest," or, "Thank You for being with me," but eventually try to be more specific.

- "Thank You, Lord, that yesterday a friend called when I was feeling lonely. That brightened my day."

- "Thank You, Father, that I was able to meet last month's sales quota. There were times when I thought I wasn't going to make it. But You came through, helping me persevere and opening my eyes to possible contacts, and I'm grateful."

- "Thank you, dear God, for helping me deal with that irate customer yesterday. I'm glad I was able to diffuse her anger."

Open your eyes to God's handiwork: a scenic view, a sunset, a sunrise, a body of water, the stars at night, a stately tree, or a flower in bloom. As you gaze on this, voice thanks for what you see, and see what will happen to you and to your praying.

I surprised myself one morning when I thanked God that the sun came up! It was a morning when I was physically tired. Consequently, my mind was sluggish and my spirit dull. As I sat in silence looking to the east through the patio door, the sun in all its bright orangeness came up. Its rays streaked across the sky, filling it with color. Color entered my own soul as it occurred to me that I had never once thanked God for this marvel, and so I did. "Thank You, Creator God, for the sun. Thank You for the dependableness of its coming up every morning. Thank You for the many blessings that have come from the sunlight. Thank You for the promise it brings for this day before me." I moved on then to pray for other things, my mental sluggishness gone and my spirit enlivened. The thought of God's dependableness stayed with me throughout the day, alerting me to other things that I had taken for granted. I marveled at His presence and His providence.

Coat every request with thanksgiving. To relate every experience to God doesn't mean you won't have requests and petitions. But even those can be said with thanks, enhancing His presence in your life and bringing peace to your heart and mind (Philippians 4:6–7).

- "Father, I am having trouble with Gina. You know how she is, so strident. I want to love and help her through these difficult teen years. I'm trusting that You are going to help me. I thank You for the patience You are going to give me and for the insight You will give me concerning her behavior."

- "Father God, my wife and I are having difficulty managing our income. I've made an appointment with a credit counselor. I pray he will be able to help us, and I thank You that You are going to give us solutions through him."

Spend time with children. When Jesus took the little children into His arms to bless them, He said to the disciples, "The kingdom of God belongs to such as these. . . . anyone who will not receive the kingdom of God like a little child will never enter it" (Mark 10:14–15). The same could be said for entering the kingdom of prayer. A rich and full prayer life belongs to those who have hearts as trusting, as dependent, as honest, as eager, as full of wonder as little children's.

Beatrice, a prolific writer, prided herself on keeping a strict schedule for herself and her child. One day though, in early spring, a friend, Laverne, persuaded her to go with her to a campground where she needed to check on some details. It was an unusually warm day, with the daffodils in bloom, so Beatrice let Jimmy, her eighteen-month-old, walk around and explore without "no-no's" while Laverne met with the camp director. Beatrice said:

> I followed Jimmy at a distance, watching my firstborn explore the world on his sea legs. He hadn't been walking long. As I followed him, I saw the world anew through his eyes. In the everyday world of work and meeting deadlines, I had forgotten the beauty of a flower, the wonder of damp rocks, the mystery of a feather blowing in the breeze, the joy of walking, and the fun of exploring. Suddenly, I was aware of God everywhere, and my heart filled with praise.

Who knows, when you practice some of these exercises, gratitude may so characterize your prayer life that it is what your friends will associate with you.

- "What a grateful prayer he is."
- "Have you noticed how she relates everything to God?"
- "Her praying is so childlike—and have you noticed how strong her faith is?"

• "I've observed that he never asks God for anything without also saying thanks in one way or the other."

Regardless, through cultivating a grateful heart, you will provide fertile soil for growing a rich prayer life because you recognize God's presence and power. You will know what Jesus knew: Nothing is too good to happen in the same world with God!

making the CONNECTION

How is a sense of wonder related to a grateful heart?

What is one way I can work on developing a grateful heart like Jesus'?

Notes

1. This passage, down to the quote of Luke 24:31, is a paraphrase of Luke 24:17–29.

2. Matthew 14:13–21; Matthew 15:32–39; Mark 6:30–44; Luke 9:10–17; John 6:1–14.

3. Mark 8:1–10.

4. This incident is also told in Matthew 19:13–15 and Luke 18:15–17.

5. William David Spencer and Aída Besançon Spencer, *The Prayer Life of Jesus: Shout of Agony, Revelation of Love, A Commentary* (Lanham, Md.: Univ. Press of America, 1990), 153.

thanks in advance

Then Jesus looked up and said, "Father, I thank you that you have heard me. I knew that you always hear me. . . .

When he had said this, Jesus called in a loud voice, "Lazarus, come out!"

—John 11:41–42, 43

Usually we think of giving thanks as coming after God has blessed us. We admonish each other to make sure we thank God for the good things He does for us, but in three incidents, Jesus thanked God before the fact of God's blessing.

the feeding of the five thousand

Do you remember how the relentless crowd pursued Jesus and the apostles when they were trying to find a place to be alone?[1] As they crossed the Sea of Galilee by boat to get to the more sparsely inhabited eastern shore, thousands of people ran around the northern end of the sea. They were waiting for Jesus when He and His friends arrived.

Out of compassion for this crowd of over five thousand people, Jesus rearranged His plans. He taught the people, healed their sick, and expressed concern about their hunger. He asked Philip, who was from the eastern shore, "Where shall we buy bread for these people to eat?" (John 6:5).

After rapid mental calculation, Philip replied, "Eight months' wages would not buy enough bread for each one to have a bite!" (v. 7).

As the day began to wear away, the apostles became anxious about the situation. Lunchtime had long passed, and the sun was beginning to set. "The disciples came to him and said, 'This is a remote place, and it's already getting late. Send the crowds away, so they can go to the villages and buy themselves some food'" (Matthew 14:15).

"Jesus replied, 'They do not need to go away. You give them something to eat'" (v. 16).

"They said to him, 'That would take eight months of a man's wages! Are we to go and spend that much on bread and give it to them to eat?'

"'How many loaves do you have?' he asked. 'Go and see'" (Mark 6:37–38).

As they looked around, they discovered a boy present who had five loaves of barley bread and two fish and reported this to Jesus. Andrew who spotted the boy was skeptical, "How far will five small barley loaves and two small fish go among so many?"

Jesus said, "Bring the loaves and fish to me."

"And he directed the people to sit down on the grass. Taking the five loaves and the two fish and *looking up to heaven, he gave thanks* and broke the loaves. Then he gave them to the disciples, and the disciples gave them to the people. They all ate and were satisfied, and the disciples picked up twelve basketfuls of broken pieces that were left over" (Matthew 14:19–20, italics added).

THE FEEDING OF THE FOUR THOUSAND

A few months later, when Jesus and His disciples were in a Gentile area, He healed a deaf and mute man.[2] As the news of this wonderful miracle spread, people gathered around Jesus, bringing their lame, blind, mute, maimed, and sick to Him (Matthew 15:29–30).

The crowds grew larger and larger until there were over four thousand people present. A "camp meeting" atmosphere prevailed. With their knapsacks and lunch baskets, they settled in to hear every word and see every miracle. "The people were amazed when they saw the mute speaking, the crippled made well, the lame walking and the blind seeing. And they praised the God of Israel" (v. 31). The Gentiles had never witnessed anything like this, and they were captivated. They hung on and would not leave, exhausting their supply of food.

Jesus was touched deeply by their needs. He called His disciples to Him and said, "I feel sorry for the crowd; they have been with me for three days now, and they have nothing to eat. I don't want to send them away, for if I send them away hungry to their own houses they may collapse on the way, for some of them are from a long distance."

The disciples were incredulous. "Where could we get enough bread in this remote place to feed such a crowd?" (Matthew 15:33).

"'How many loaves do you have?' Jesus asked.

"'Seven,' they replied.

"He told the crowd to sit down on the ground. When he had taken the seven loaves and *given thanks,* he broke them and gave them to his disciples to set before the people, and they did so. They had a few small fish as well; he *gave thanks for them also* and told the disciples to distribute them. The people ate and were satisfied. Afterward the disciples picked up seven basketfuls of broken pieces that were left over" (Mark 8:5–8, italics added).

THE RAISING OF LAZARUS

Some months later, when Jesus and his disciples were in Perea, another Gentile area, word came to Him of the grave illness of his friend Lazarus, the brother of Martha and Mary in Bethany of Judea.

Jesus and His disciples went to Bethany. Martha and Mary were upset with Jesus because by the time He arrived, Lazarus had died. Each said to Him, "If you had been here, my brother would not have died" (John 11:21, 32). Mourners who had gathered felt the same way: "Could not he who opened the eyes of the blind man have kept this man from dying?" (v. 37).

Jesus went to the tomb, a cave with a stone laid across the entrance. He said, "Take away the stone."

Martha protested, "But, Lord, by this time there is a bad odor, for he has been there four days" (v. 39).

Nevertheless, the stone was removed. "Then Jesus looked up and said, *'Father, I thank you that you have heard me'*" (v. 41, italics added).

Then Jesus called loudly, "Lazarus, come out!" (v. 43), and he did. The dead man was now alive.

On each of these three occasions, Jesus gave thanks in advance before any visible evidence occurred. With eyes of faith, He could see God answering. The disciples and Mary and Martha didn't see possibilities. Reality ruled.

SEEING THE IMPOSSIBLE

Jesus gave thanks in circumstances that appeared almost impossible to solve. At least His disciples and Mary and Martha saw it that way.

The disciples' view. When Jesus had pity on the crowds, and when He wanted to give them something to eat, the disciples immediately pointed out the practical difficulties.

• They were in isolated, sparsely settled areas.

- There was nowhere within miles where any food could be obtained.
- If there were food, the cost would be too much.

Martha and Mary's view. Lazarus had been buried, and all hope was gone out of the hearts of his sisters. Both were upset with Jesus, insisting that if He had been there Lazarus would not have died. Their friends who shared their grief thought the same thing. They were all aware that Jesus was a miracle worker.

Even after Jesus explained the possibility of resurrection in the here and now (John 11:25), Martha still didn't grasp it. When Jesus ordered the stone removed from the tomb's entrance, she said, "But, Lord, . . . by this time there is a bad odor, for he has been there four days" (v. 39). Facts were facts.

In contrast to the disciples and to Mary and Martha, Jesus saw possibilities, and He thanked God as if they were facts. His thanks in advance was a powerful expression of faith. Faith overshadowed impossibilities. Nothing was too good to happen in the same world as God, and His actions showed it.

faith at work

When the disciples insisted they didn't have any way to feed so many people, Jesus insisted that resources were present. He said to His disciples, "What do you have? Go and look." When they found a few fish and loaves, they saw the amount as very small and insignificant compared to the size of the crowds. Nevertheless, in Jesus' eyes they were enough if given to God. While everybody else was wringing their hands, Jesus took the loaves and fish, calmly looked up to heaven, and gave thanks. He was so confident that He organized the crowds for distribution. He told the disciples to pass the food around, and what was little became more than enough to feed thousands of people.

Jesus offered no prayer of petition at the feedings of the multitudes; neither did He at Lazarus' tomb, although petition was probably involved in Jesus' resurrection. In His prayer, Jesus said, "Father, I thank you that you have heard me" (John 11:41), meaning that sometime earlier He had prayed for Lazarus. He was certain that God had heard Him and that God would respond. *The Interpreter's Bible* says that His prayer of thanks was so audaciously believing, it burst through the usual limitations and brought Lazarus from the dead.[2]

Is there a chance we could become audacious believers? Could we have the kind of faith that could offer thanks in advance, as Jesus did? Some might readily answer "Yes!" while others might be doubtful, since the circumstances seemed so impossible and the results were so phenomenal. We might be tempted to dismiss the feeding of the five thousand, the feeding of the four thousand, and the raising of Lazarus as great stories that have no applicability for *our* prayer lives. Yet I do not think this is the way Jesus would want us to respond. When He prayed at the tomb of Lazarus, He said, "I said this for the benefit of the people standing here" (v. 42). There was something inherent in the situation that He wanted the people to learn. He wanted Lazarus' friends and relatives to believe that God had sent Him, and I believe He wants us to learn from this experience, too, and we can, if we identify with Him.

POINT of IDENTITY

In chapter 1, we mentioned the importance of feeling a kinship with Jesus in order to learn from Him. With the first cornerstone, solitude, that wasn't hard to do; whether we practice it or not, most of us sense the need for withdrawing for prayer. But the miraculous feedings and the raising of Lazarus are just too unusual for me to identify with. Although I've asked God to stretch a meal when unexpected company arrives, I'm too rational to see how five loaves and two fish could stretch to feed thousands of people. I wouldn't even consider it. Neither have I stood at a casket or at a grave and asked God to bring a person back to life; if I did and you heard me, you would consider me weird.

I'll admit, though, that from time to time all of us find our-selves in situations that look *to us* as impossible as the feeding of the five thousand and of the four thousand and the raising of Lazarus. It may be the size of the problem—it is too big to solve. It may be the severity—it's too complicated. It may be our view of the situation—if we are pessimists at heart. An opti-mist would see the situation differently, so what appears impos-sible will vary from person to person.

While writing this book, I came up against a situation I regarded as impossible, although I'm certain others would not see it that way. I believed God had given me a vision for a par-ticipatory type of retreat for women, and I wanted to see this vision become reality. Some women agreed to help me plan it, and three even helped me pay the deposit for the retreat cen-ter. At no time, though, did we discuss what we would do if we didn't have sufficient enrollment to meet the final bill of over four thousand dollars. We had a "puppy love" kind of faith—not really thinking long-term, just giddy with the belief in a vision. As we launched the publicity, we wrote a small article for the local newspaper, hoping for some coverage in the *Lifestyle* section. We ended up with a large front-page article—we couldn't have asked for better coverage. I thought, *If any-thing will do it, this will bring in the women.*

But it didn't. Not only did no one register, no one even called to inquire. *If no one responded to that kind of publicity,* I won-dered, *would anyone respond?* That led to, *How in the world will I ever pay the bill?* And it would be me because I was the one who initiated the retreat and my name was on the con-tract for the retreat center. Obviously—I can say this now—this situation wasn't hopeless, but it *felt* hopeless to me. The size of the problem so dominated my attention that I couldn't see solutions. Fear and anxiety took over.

In *The Light Within You,* John Claypool wrote, "Fear has a way of making us shortsighted and reducing our field of vision. Again and again, in the face of problems, I have been totally one-sided in my outlook and conceive the situation as utterly barren of positive possibilities. But, as Jesus demonstrated when he fed the five thousand [and the four thousand], such a way of looking at things is simply unrealistic! It denies the presence of God in all that he has created."[3] There are always some loaves and fishes "in the midst of every problem, if we only have eyes to see."[4]

OPENING OUR EYES TO SEE

When the disciples insisted they didn't have anything to feed the crowd with, Jesus said, "Go and see." In other words, do some investigation. *What were the loaves and fishes in my situation?* I had to search with pencil and paper because fear and anxiety so dominated my thoughts that thinking about resources made little impact. Here's my list.

- *Time*. The retreat was still six months away. The bill wasn't due tomarrow. There were still many publicity options.
- *Vision*. God had given me the desire for the retreat. I was not acting on a whim. If God had initiated it, surely He would lead women to come.
- *Partners*. Enthusiastic women had committed themselves to planning the retreat with me. Although I was responsible for the bill, they would all be working very hard.
- *Power.* We had the power of minds working together and of prayer. I could pray more, and I could ask others to pray. I was so thankful to be writing a book on prayer, and especially this chapter. What a chance to put into practice what I was writing!

As you can tell by that exclamation mark, my mood perked up. Developing a list of resources is a hope-raiser and a faith-builder. "Awareness becomes the basis of hope, and hope becomes the basis of courage and confidence, and it all goes back to the discipline of gratitude when we choose 'to count our blessings, name them one by one,' and be astonished all over again, not just at what God has done, but what He can be counted on to do in the future."5

faith for the future

For many, recognizing the resources inherent in your what-appears-to-be-impossible situation may be all you need to pray as Jesus did. You take your resources, give them to God, and say, "Thank you, God, for what you are going to do." Like Jesus, you still can't see the evidence, but your prayer is an act of faith.

Others, though, may still find saying thanks in advance believingly and confidently—where it is really an act of faith—challenging. Here are some ways we can strengthen our faith.

Thank God for hearing prayers. If you can't say thanks in advance, then build your trust in God by thanking Him for hearing our prayers. We can take Jesus' prayer, "I thank You that You always hear me," and make it our prayer. This is a wonderfully reassuring sentence to verbalize in our prayers.

Thank God that He is going to respond. As you pray, say, "God, I thank You that even now You are working to answer my request," or, "I thank You that You are hearing my prayer and You are beginning now to answer." When the man from God appeared to Daniel in a vision, he said, "Do not be afraid, Daniel. Since the first day that you set your mind to gain understanding and to humble yourself before your God, your words were heard, and I have come in response to them" (Daniel 10:12). The man of God had been detained for twenty-one days, but Daniel's prayer had been heard immediately.

Give thanks for the items on your resource list. I took the items on my list of resources and gave thanks for them.

"Thank You, Lord, for the vision You gave me.
Thank You, Lord, for the women You gave me to work with.
Thank You, Lord, for the opportunity to grow in my faith.

Thank You that I am writing a book on prayer that encourages me."

These became prayers that I said on my daily walks. The more I prayed, the less anxious I became and the brighter the future looked.

Act in faith. One of Jesus' staggering prayer promises is "Whatever you ask for in prayer, believe that you have received it, and it will be yours" (Mark 11:24). What actions would you take if you really believed God was going to provide a miraculous solution to your impossible situation? Then take those actions such as Jesus took at Lazarus' tomb and when feeding the multitudes. He ordered the stone removed even when Martha protested. He organized the crowds and told the disciples to distribute what they had. He took these actions before tangible answers were in sight. Now I don't believe Jesus did these things to build His faith, but we can take decisive actions like these to boost ours. As I thanked God for the resources I had and for hearing my prayers, I also continued to promote the retreat, engage discussion leaders, and have planning meetings. Although I couldn't yet say a confident, "Thanks in advance," I could move ahead with *some* faith and trust Him for the results.

When we are faced with situations that appear to us as impossible, we can take what faith we have and build on it through gratitude and actions until the day comes when we can say thanks in advance and mean it. Although we want to always say thanks for past blessings, we also want to trust God so much that we can say thanks before He answers. We want to be audacious believers who see marvelous results!

making the
CONNECTION

Am I more likely to see possibilities or impossibilities in a troubling situation?

What is one way I can work toward becoming an audacious believer?

Notes

1. The description here is a compilation of the four accounts of this incident as it appears in Matthew 14:13–21; Mark 6:30–44; Luke 9:10–17; and John 6:1–15.

2. *The Interpreter's Bible* (Nashville: Abingdon, 1955), 8:642.

3. John R. Claypool, *The Light Within You* (Waco, Tex.: Word, 1983), 117–18.

4. Ibid.

5. John R. Claypool, "Anxiety, Gratitude and Trust," a sermon delivered at Northminster Baptist Church, Jackson, Mississippi, 23 November 1980.

the trusting side of thanks

"I praise Thee, O Father, Lord of heaven and earth, that Thou didst hide these things from the wise and intelligent and didst reveal them to babes.

"Yes, Father, for thus it was well-pleasing in Thy sight."
—Matthew 11:25–26; Luke 10:21 NASB 1977

You are driving south on a four-lane highway with a wide grassy median. Traffic is moving well, and you're glad because you're groggy from lack of sleep. You're half-listening to the radio announcer when you suddenly become wide awake. A car from a northbound lane is in the median, coming toward you. You hit your anti-lock brakes just in time. The car crosses the southbound lanes right in front of you, and you feel enormous relief. As soon as you can, you pull over so you can check on the driver in the out-of-control car. It is now resting on its side in a ditch. All the while, you are breathing thanks. "Oh, Father, thank You that the car missed me. Thank You that I am alive."

After your annual mammogram, your doctor calls. She tells you that a spot showed up on your X ray so you need to return to the hospital for a second X ray. She doesn't say the word cancer, but it lodges itself in your thoughts. After the second X ray, you are called again. A third X ray and a sonogram are taken. Finally, the radiologist says, "I have good news for you. You do not have cancer. What we thought was a lump is a harmless cyst. You are OK." You walk out of the hospital feeling very grateful. "Thank You, God; thank You that I do not have cancer."

You and your spouse have been praying faithfully for your wayward daughter to return home. You both grieve about the tension that prompted her to finally say, "I'm outta here." You've wondered about her so much. Where is she? How is she taking care of herself? Will she come back home? Two very long weeks go by before you finally get a phone call. She says, "I want to come home. Can you come and get me?" Hurriedly, you get in the car. As you drive, your gratitude spills out with all the jubilation that the father of the prodigal son had when his child came home. "Father, I am ready to roast the fatted calf! Thank You that my child is coming home."

We can understand and relate to the gratitude expressed on these occasions. We would feel the same way, but what if the scenarios had turned out differently? The cars collide, and you suffer severe injuries. The diagnosis is cancer. Your daughter does not return home. Could you express thanksgiving then? Can you express gratitude to God during the bad times as well as the good times, as Jesus did?

Thanks During the Good Times

During the last year of Jesus' ministry, when opposition was keen, Jesus picked seventy men (Luke 10:1 NASB; seventy-two, NIV) to go ahead of Him to Judean villages and towns. He divided them into groups of twos and instructed them.

- "Do not take a purse or bag or sandals."

- "Do not greet anyone on the road."

- "When you enter a house, say, 'Peace to this house.'"

- "When you stay in a house, eat and drink whatever is given you."

- "Heal the sick."

- "Tell everyone 'The kingdom of God is near you.'"

- "When you are not welcomed in a town, tell the residents they will suffer consequences for their behavior."

Jesus added a forceful illustration from His own ministry of the consequences to those who rejected them. He referred to the dreadful fate of the Galilean towns of Korazin, Bethsaida, and Capernaum, who would be punished severely for rejecting Him. To the seventy, Jesus said, "The one who listens to you listens to Me, and the one who rejects you rejects Me; and he who rejects Me rejects the One who sent Me" (Luke 10:16 NASB).

After such somber instructions, perhaps the seventy didn't have high expectations about their mission, so when they were successful, they were elated. To their surprise, they found that people listened, healings occurred, and demons submitted to them in the name of Jesus.

You can almost see Jesus smiling as they reported their triumphs. He said, "I saw Satan fall like lightning from heaven" (v. 18 NIV). Actually, their success was only a tiny dent in the mass of evil in the world, but with His sense of wonder, Jesus saw it as prophetic of the final and complete quick-as-lightning downfall of Satan, the chief of demons, that would one day occur. Seeing this glorious future was an occasion of holy joy for Jesus.

The Bible says, "At that very time He rejoiced greatly in the Holy Spirit" (Luke 10:21 NASB), but *rejoiced* is far too colorless a translation for the Greek *egalliasato*.[1] It means a positive exultation or thrilled with joy. In His elation, Jesus prayed. In the King James Version, His prayer begins with "I thank thee, O Father" (Luke 10:21). In the *New American Standard Bible,* it is "I praise You, O Father." The sentence "carries the idea of continual open praise. An expanded translation might well read, 'I continuously and openly confess and exalt Thee.'"[2]

He goes on to say, "Thou didst hide these things from the wise and intelligent and didst reveal them to babes. Yes, Father, for thus it was well-pleasing in Thy sight" (v. 21 NASB 1977). The joyous report of the seventy triggered a spontaneous and highly emotional response in Christ, and He burst forth in praise.

This was a lovely prayer said at a time of joy, and Jesus said this exact same prayer at a time when things weren't so joyful.

thanks during the hard times

Jesus experienced His greatest popularity and largest followings in Galilee, but this doesn't mean everyone enthusiastically embraced Him. The people of Korazin, Bethsaida, and Capernaum—the same cities mentioned above—simply disregarded Jesus. Even though most of His mighty works were done in these three Galilean cities, the residents did not repent. How did Jesus react? He upbraided the three cities and He gave thanks (Matthew 11:20–26).

He compared Korazin and Bethsaida to the wicked heathen cities of Tyre and Sidon. If those cities had witnessed the dynamic works of Jesus, they would have repented. They would have used sackcloth and ashes, as did citizens of Nineveh when they repented following Jonah's preaching (Jonah 3:5–9). He said, "I assure you that on the Judgment Day, God will show more mercy to the people of Tyre and Sidon than to you!" (see Matthew 11:22).

Capernaum not only witnessed Jesus' miracles and heard His preaching, but He had lived there. Jesus compared Capernaum with the very worst city He could have chosen, Sodom, a city noted for its iniquity. If the dynamic manifestations of power seen by the people of Capernaum had been witnessed by the people living in Sodom, that city would not have been destroyed by fire. It would still be in existence. Jesus added, "You can be sure that on the Judgment Day God will show more mercy to Sodom than to Capernaum!" (see v. 24).

The accent in Jesus' voice as He pronounced woes on the three cities is one of anger and sorrowful pity. It is "the accent of one who offered men the most precious thing in the world, and who saw it completely disregarded; the accent of one who is watching a tragedy being played out, and who is powerless to stop men rushing on ruin. . . . Jesus' condemnation of sin is holy anger, but the anger comes, not from outraged pride, but from a broken heart."[3]

There's no joy and jubilation here as there was when the seventy returned; nevertheless, Jesus gave thanks. "I praise Thee, O Father, Lord of heaven and earth, that Thou didst hide these things from the wise and intelligent and didst reveal them to babes. Yes, Father, for thus it was well-pleasing in Thy sight" (vv. 25–26 NASB 1977).

"The Galilean towns might be blind to the true nature of Jesus and the significance of His actions. But Jesus Himself, so far from feeling personal resentment, thanked God that there were some, for the most part the less sophisticated and the less important, who turned instinctively to Him."[4]

Jesus' expressing gratitude when He was rejected adds another dimension to the cornerstone of thanksgiving—the trusting side of thanks. The fact that Jesus prayed this prayer when He was being rejected reveals trust. He trusted God and God's ways. The rejection of Him by privileged people did not thwart God's purposes. The less sophisticated and humble people welcomed Him and responded to His message. God's will was still being accomplished.

In the previous two chapters, we were encouraged by Jesus' example to relate everything to its Ultimate Source and to make thanksgiving an act of faith. Now His example is inviting us to add another dimension. Can we develop the trusting side of thanks? Can we give God thanks during hard times? This is something we may resist doing, and here's why.

REASONS FOR RESISTANCE

We suspect that it was easy for Jesus to give thanks because He just seemed to burst forth in praise to God. Even though He was praying in public, there was no "let us pray" preliminary. The words just rolled off His tongue. When difficult things happen to us, we don't feel thankful. Instead we may feel angry, hurt, confused, sorrowful, sad, or frustrated. We may ask questions: *Why me? Why did this have to happen? Where is God?* We may be plagued by negative thoughts, as if we are walking in a fog.

Our spiritual vision and outlook on life are clouded. We may find it hard to cope. Nothing of what we are experiencing is conducive to giving thanks, so words of praise don't leap out of our mouths. If they are going to come, they are going to have to be forced out—and wouldn't that be hypocritical or dishonest?

Saying thanks without *feeling* grateful is not hypocritical or dishonest when it is an exercise of trust. Trust means going ahead and saying thanks when you don't feel like it. Trusting thanks is based on God's nature and not on our feelings. Jesus' prayer was about God, His sovereignty, and His perspective, and that's where our focus is to be.

In addition to resisting because we don't feel thankful, some may also resist because of the seriousness of their situation. Whereas the rejection Jesus experienced was extensive, coming from three cities, we may feel it really doesn't compare with the pain we are experiencing. What is rejection compared to cancer, crippling injuries, a debilitating disease, a lost daughter, or a wayward son?

I'm sympathetic to this reason for resisting, so much so that I had difficulty writing this chapter, yet Jesus' example invites us to exercise trust by giving God thanks during difficult times. Paul must have had Jesus' example in mind when he wrote, "Be joyful always; pray continually; give thanks in all circumstances, for this is God's will for you in Christ Jesus" (1 Thessalonians 5:16–18).

If we cannot bring ourselves to say thanks for the difficult situation, perhaps we can find something in it that we can be thankful for. "What we face in a given situation is not all light or all darkness, total goodness or total evil, but a baffling mixture of light and darkness, goodness and evil, factors that are going for us and factors that are going against us."[5]

Recognizing the complexity of our situation, we can exercise trust by acknowledging specific things in our situation to thank God for. Ask yourself, *What is there here to be thankful for? What can be salvaged from this experience? What can I learn? What can I use to build toward the future?* Then use the answers to your questions as items to be thankful for.

For example, practically any circumstance can be used by God to shape us into the character of Christ. "I thank You God that You are shaping me into the character of Christ, and for that shaping, I am grateful. For so it seemed good in Your sight."

Virtually any suffering can be a way for us to experience "the fellowship of sharing in his sufferings" (Philippians 3:10) so that we may know Christ more intimately. "Thank You, God, for this time of suffering. Now I understand more what Jesus went through and feel closer to Him. I have a greater consciousness of His love, and I thank You for that."

In a lighter vein, when Matthew Henry, author of a set of Bible commentaries, was robbed of his life's savings, he prayed, "I thank thee first because I was never robbed before; second, because although they took my purse, they did not take my life; third, although they took all, it was not much; and, fourth, because it was I who was robbed and not I who robbed." There's always something to be thankful for in every situation. And it's there that we can begin exercising our trust. When we do, what will be the results?

WHEN WE CHOOSE TO TRUST

For Sandie, being thankful in all things stretched her, but she worked at it. In the process she grew in her capacity to trust God. She wrote:

119

If I had a flat tire, I would thank God that it was in my drive-way rather than on some deserted stretch of road or that it hadn't been a blow-out on the highway, etc. But God started convicting me that I was thanking Him around the situation—not for the situation itself. As I began to meditate on this con-cept, He pointed out to me that He would not have permitted these particular situations unless they could perfect me. They were refining fire. They actually were answers to prayers, for I had been praying for a deeper walk and to be a purer vessel. Rather than thanking God for not allowing trouble to be worse than it was, I began to thank Him for the trouble itself, includ-ing a cancer scare with my son. He had a tumor, and as we waited for the report from the biopsy, I dropped to my knees and thanked God. If it was going to be cancer, I thanked Him for finding us worthy to undergo this test. I thanked Him for the opportunity to testify to people who we would not be able to minister to otherwise. I thanked Him for the lessons we would learn as a result.

As I began to apply thankfulness to every difficult situation, I noticed the tables turned. The situations were resolved in incredible ways, including my son's tumor being benign. It was almost as if a bubble of blessing descended over us.

When my friend Debbie was a missionary in Senegal, she often experienced exhaustion, loneliness, and frustration that would make her wish she were somewhere else—anyplace but in Senegal. She said:

> At those times I would go up on the roof at night. It was cooler there, and since there were no or few lights, the sky was gor-geous. I could watch people passing by, and I thanked God for them. I could watch family and friends mingling as they brought their animals home for the night. I thanked God for relation-ships, for laughter and love. When I started thanking God for one thing, it would lead to thanking Him for other things. In that atmosphere of thankfulness, heaven opened, and God reminded me why I was there. He had called me. I was in Senegal

because that was His place for me, and I realized what a privilege it was to serve God. My focus changed from how miserable I was to how I could better serve Him. My situation did not change but my attitude did when I gave thanks.

Debbie could have said, "Well, I'm here; I'm stuck. I'll just have to be miserable until my time is up." Jesus could have said, "Well, let people be people. If they choose to reject Me, that's their problem." But He didn't. He responded with thanksgiving and consequently was able to see God in His circumstances. His conclusion was that what He was experiencing was well pleasing in God's sight.

Once we begin to practice thanksgiving during difficult times, we can begin to see the possibility of purpose behind the circumstances and the possibility of good coming out of what we are enduring. Perhaps in some mysterious way God is accomplishing something that we can't begin to fathom with our limited understanding and limited view.

Our view changes—our view of God and the circumstances. The weightiness of the problem lightens as we realize, *This situation isn't as bad as I thought it was.* We begin to see how we can cope with our situation. We no longer feel like a victim; rather, we feel more like a victor. There is something we can do. We are not helpless.

Our mood changes; hope rises. Our thinking becomes more positive. Gary Thomas, writing in *Moody* magazine, said, "I like to think of thankfulness as God's 'spiritual air freshener.' It replaces the stale odor of resentment with a sweeter-smelling perfume."[6]

When we select the trust option, we experience various benefits: spiritual growth, altered circumstances, bubbles of blessings, heaven opening, courage to conquer, and fresher air. Giving thanks during difficult times is a powerful tool, but it is not a panacea—a remedy that works every time for all the difficulties we experience. Our lives are complex. Our prayer needs vary. Sometimes we may need other tools to help us cope with difficult situations, such as being honest about our feelings.

This is something we will learn more about as we study the next cornerstone in Jesus' prayer life: being honest with God.

making the
CONNECTION

How would my praying change if I knew God were completely trustworthy?

In my current situation, what is one thing I can be thankful for?

Notes

1. Leon Morris, *The Gospel According to St. Luke,* Tyndale New Testament Commentaries vol. 3, (Grand Rapids: Eerdmans, 1974), 184–86.

2. Curtis C. Mitchell, *Praying Jesus' Way* (Old Tappan, N.J.: Revell, 1977), 25.

3. William Barclay, *The Gospel of Matthew,* 2d ed., vol. 2, The Daily Study Bible (Edinburgh: Saint Andrew, 1958, 1965), 13.

4. R. V. G. Tasker, *The Gospel According to St. Matthew,* Tyndale New Testament Commentaries, vol. 1 (Grand Rapids: Eerdmans, 1961), 121.

5. John R. Claypool, "Anxiety, Gratitude, and Trust," a sermon delivered at Broadway Baptist Church, Fort Worth, Tex., 23 November 1975.

6. Gary Thomas, "Giving Thanks," *Moody,* November-December 1996, 59.

PART THREE

Honesty

the HONest struggle of a troubled heart

"Now my heart is troubled, and what shall I say? 'Father, save me from this hour'? No, it was for this very reason I came to this hour. Father, glorify your name!"

—John 12:27

Most people experience tension at some time or other. The events in our lives, our responsibilities, the time crunches we experience, the expectations we have of ourselves, and the expectations we sense others have of us wrap around us. The stress of the outside wrappings forces a pressure buildup within. As we heave a huge sigh, we wonder, *Did Jesus experience tension and inner pressure? Surely not. He probably moved through life like a phantom, completely unscathed by what was happening around Him or by what others thought.*

That kind of thinking is natural for a person wrapped in stress. Accomplishment always looks easier for the other person, and especially someone like Jesus. From where we stand, Jesus' triumph is so certain that it looks effortless and without strain. His courage is so calm, so sure, so seemingly inevitable, that it looks automatic. Because He is the Son of God, with all the resources of heaven on His side, we're tempted to think He must have been immune from emotional and mental strain. What we have seen so far of His prayer life—particularly His need for solitude—has shown us otherwise. We'll see further evidence of the strain Jesus experienced as we look at the cornerstone of honesty.

The closer Jesus got to the cross, the greater the emotional and mental strain, and He found relief by being honest with God. He didn't hesitate to admit He had a troubled heart during times of tension.

TENSION-PRODUCING EVENTS

The streets of Jerusalem were filled with people mingling and talking as Passover neared.[1] They were wondering if Jesus would come. "They asked one another, 'What do you think? Isn't he coming to the Feast at all?' But the chief priests and Pharisees had given orders that if anyone found out where Jesus was, he should report it so that they might arrest him" (John 11:56b–57). From the time Jesus brought Lazarus back to life, they had been planning to kill Jesus. Jesus had withdrawn to the desert to avoid capture, but as the Passover neared, He courageously headed toward Jerusalem.

When He got near Jerusalem on Friday afternoon, He went to see Mary, Martha, and Lazarus in Bethany. Word spread that He was there. People from Jerusalem came to see Him and to see Lazarus. Lazarus' miraculous comeback was drawing people to Jesus, and this alarmed the chief priests, so they made plans to kill Lazarus (12:10–11). To have His friend's life threatened added stress to Jesus' already complicated situation.

When Jesus went into Jerusalem on Sunday, the streets were lined with people. They were excited. Jesus was coming! They spread their cloaks on the road and waved branches of palm trees, receiving Him like the conqueror they wanted Him to be. They shouted, "Praise God! God bless Him who comes in the name of the Lord!"

Jesus rode in on a donkey, a symbol that He was not the conqueror they wanted Him to be. Rather He was on a peaceful mission. No one saw it that way, not even the disciples, causing Jesus to be grieved. He wept over Jerusalem. He said, "If you, even you, had only known on this day what would bring you peace—but now it is hidden from your eyes" (Luke 19:41–42).

Jesus went to the temple. He healed needy people, the blind, and the lame (Matthew 21:14). Little children sang, "Hosanna to the Son of David" (v. 15) while Jewish authorities watched with arms crossed and scowling faces. Their eyes were livid with anger.

On Monday, Jesus went back to the temple. Outraged by what He saw there, He knocked over the tables of the money-changers and the stalls of those selling sacrificial animals. As He drove out the merchants and their customers, He said, "[The Scriptures declare], 'My house will be called a house of prayer,' but you are making it a 'den of robbers'" (v. 13).

The chief priests, the scribes, and other leaders were furious. Who did Jesus think He was to disrupt business? He had no authority to do what He did. They were afraid to do anything, though, because Jesus was popular among the common people. They hung on every word He said.

Perhaps it was the words of Jesus' teaching that attracted some Greeks who were in town for Passover. They came to Philip and Andrew and said, "We would like to see Jesus" (John 12:21). Philip and Andrew had no way of knowing, but the Greeks' request was pregnant with meaning for Jesus. It was a signal to Him that His "hour" had come.

Previously, when Jesus had spoken of His "hour" (John 2:4; 7:6, 30; 8:20 KJV, NASB; "time," NIV), He indicated that it had not yet come. He had also said that He would lay down His life (10:11, 15) and that other sheep not belonging to the fold (the Gentiles) would join His flock (v. 16). The request of the Greeks was a signal that it was time for that to happen. To bring the Greeks in required His death (12:24). He would not be a military conqueror who would subject the kingdoms of the world under His feet. Instead, He would be glorified through death. He underscored this by saying that only by death comes life; only by spending life do we retain it, and only by service comes greatness (vv. 25–26).

It is one matter to say these things; it is another to be the life that gives itself, to be the seed that dies in the ground. The stark reality of His imminent death mingled with the hostility of His enemies, the pull of people who needed Him, and the frustration of being misunderstood produced a troubled heart. How did Jesus handle this?

a SHORt, HONeSt pRAyeR

As the pressure built up, Jesus must have wanted to withdraw from the crowd. He must have longed for the relief and refreshment He had found in lonely places on other stressful occasions. But He was not alone. He was surrounded by people (John 12:29). Not being able to escape, Jesus did the next best thing. He prayed where He was. Right in the middle of people who did not fully understand Him and, therefore, were not sympathetic to His needs, Jesus said, "Now my heart is troubled, and what shall I say? 'Father, save me from this hour'? No, it was for this very reason I came to this hour. Father, glorify your name!" (John 12:27–28).

In the *New International Version,* His prayer has thirty-two words. The *New American Standard Version* has thirty words. I don't usually count the words of prayers, but the shortness of this prayer in light of the complexity of the situation is impressive. This observation is not to take anything away from the value we noted in Jesus' early morning prayer times or His all-night vigils. There are times when lengthy praying is important, but there are also times when just a few words will do, and this was one of those. He urgently needed to pray.

As people pressed in around Him, Jesus honestly admitted what He was feeling. His prayer was a spontaneous admission of the emotion that had been building up within Him. He didn't see what He was feeling as something to hide or to be embarrassed about; He saw it as something to be confessed.

Along with expressing His heart's condition, Jesus grappled with what to pray regarding the tension He was experiencing. On the one side was the desire to escape; on the other side was God's purpose. He already knew God willed death for Him. The dilemma was, "Should I pray for escape, or should I go on?"

Once Jesus confessed His feelings, admitting the duality of His struggle, He reiterated His basic desire, "Father, glorify your name!" (John 12:28). It was as if the confession and verbal grappling reminded Him of what was most important. In all that He said and did, He wanted to be the obedient Son so that God's power could be manifested.

Jesus' prayer was short, honest, and powerful. It was a prayer that reached heaven.

HEAVEN OPENED

Immediately after Jesus prayed, "A voice came from heaven" (John 12:28). The voice of God came to Jesus at His baptism when He first set out to do the work God had given Him to do (Mark 1:11). It came to Him on the Mount of Transfiguration when God confirmed He was headed in the right direction, toward Jerusalem and the cross (9:7). And now it came to Him when He was struggling with the tension of escape versus obedience.

The voice from heaven said, "I have glorified it, and will glorify it again" (John 12:28). God had been glorified by the work of Jesus in the past: when He taught in the synagogues; when He raised to life the widow's son at Nain; when He healed the bent woman, the leper, the blind man, and the paralytic (see Matthew 15:31; Luke 4:15; 7:16; 5:25–26; 13:13; 17:15; 18:43). God would be glorified in the future with Jesus' crucifixion (Luke 23:47; John 7:39; cf. 21:19). The crowd standing around heard the voice but was unable to distinguish what was said. Some said it was thunder, but others said an angel spoke to Jesus (John 12:29).

The voice, Jesus said, was for the people (v. 30). However, as dramatic as a voice from heaven might be, it made no significant change in the people at the time. They went right on misunderstanding (v. 34). Jesus was the one who was helped.

"Fortified by an overwhelming sense of heavenly approval, Jesus triumphantly cried, Now . . . is the judgment of this world."[2] Confidently He told them, "When I am lifted up from the earth, I will draw everyone to me."[3] The relief gained from the prayer served to steel Jesus' determination to continue toward the cross. He was certain that if He went on, something would happen which would break the power of evil once and for all. A deathblow would be struck to Satan, the ruler of this world, and Jesus' upraised, crucified figure would draw all men, Jews and Gentiles, unto Him.

What came between the tension and the triumph? Jesus' honest, sincere praying in less than perfect circumstances changed the one into the other, and this kind of praying can do the same for us. What God did for Jesus, He wants to do for every person.

PRAYING WHERE YOU ARE

In times of tension, we may put off praying because our hearts are longing for the peaceful rest that solitude provides. We want the quiet, the aloneness, the time to sort through things and listen for God's response, so we resist praying any other way. We think, *One of these mornings, I'm going to get up early and pray this through,* or *I am going to try to get away to a retreat center soon.*

Carol craved solitude after her divorce. Her biggest adjustment was accepting the total responsibility of her home and children. In addition, there were job adjustments when she became employed after a ten-year absence from the labor force. Her personal time had vanished, and she thought she was going to sink under the load. Mentally, she knew she needed divine help, but when did she have time to pray? To get up any earlier than she was now was impossible, and she was so tired when the children finally went to sleep at night that she fell exhausted into bed.

It was quite by accident that Carol discovered some time alone to pray. She was dropping her son off at school. They were having another conversation that couldn't be finished because of a lack of time. He got out of the car, looked back, and said bitterly, "Mother, we never have time to finish anything anymore." As she pulled away from the school and proceeded to work, she cried out, "Oh, God, help me. I can't bear all of this alone." It was a short, honest prayer that revealed her heart. Needs and frustration tumbled out, in no particular order. By the time she got to work, fifteen minutes later, her shoulders were lighter. There was an inner calmness and confidence as she sensed she just might be able to cope after all.

Others may put off praying because we just don't know what to say. Inside, different strands of what we are struggling with agitate like laundry in an automatic washer. They swirl around and around. We think, *If I could just figure this out, stop the churning, then I would pray and ask God to help me.*

We don't have to have an ideal environment or even know what we are going to say as long as we are honest. Jesus did not suffer in silence and hold back what He was experiencing as if He had to present some kind of "dressed-up, formal" version of Himself to God. When it comes to finding relief from the tension, it is more important *that* we pray than *how* we pray.

If you have trouble getting started, start praying with words similar to what Jesus said.

- "Father, I feel trapped because . . ."
- "Now my stomach is churning . . ."
- "My inner self is filled with pressure; I feel as if I am going to explode . . ."

If you can't unravel the stress causing your tension so that you can articulate it, then sort it out in your verbalized prayer.

- "God, I am caught between . . . On the one hand, I feel . . . But on the other hand, I want . . ."
- "Lord, I am in a vise, and the jaws are squeezing in on me. One side of the vise is . . . The other side is . . . The harder the sides squeeze, the more inner pressure I feel."
- "My soul is troubled. I'm troubled about . . . and I'm also troubled about . . . I don't even know how to pray about this, but I do know I want to do your will."

Another option is to admit our feelings and our struggle in front of a group, as Jesus did. We don't have to give a complete case history of our tension or trace all its details, although this might be therapeutic. In a Wednesday night prayer meeting, in a Sunday school class, in a Bible study, or among close friends, we might say, "The tension inside is so great I can't seem to sort out what I'm feeling. I want to do right, but I'm having trouble knowing what that is. I need you to pray with me because I want to glorify God."

Honest praying breaks up the impact of the swirling emotions and thoughts that trouble our hearts; it allows the pressure to escape. Verbalizing the tension we are experiencing diminishes its power, freeing us to pray as we ought, "Father, glorify Thy name." When the strain of life fills our heart with pressure, we can pray as we are, where we are, find relief, and reach heaven. When we make ourselves pray honestly, we'll be able to turn our tension toward triumph, as Jesus did. What we may not be able to do with a short, honest prayer, though, is eliminate the tension once and for all.

ONGOING TENSION

Short, honest praying is a tension reliever, a way to reach heaven when we think we can't pray or don't have time to pray. The relief and God's response to us will enable us to go on, but it doesn't necessarily mean an end to the tension, especially if it is related to an ongoing role, such as parenting, trying to reach a deadline, cultivating a relationship, or doing God's will.

After Carol, the woman mentioned above, discovered relief when she prayed on the way to work, she thought that was the end of her frustrations, but it wasn't. The next morning, her frustrations were back on her shoulders ready to spend the day with her. She remembered, though, the prayer of the previous morning. *It had helped. Would it help again?* She was tempted to think it wouldn't, but she made herself pray, and to her relief, the peace returned.

After that, Carol's rides to work became meaningful prayer times with the Lord. She thought of Him as her companion (which not only improved her praying, but improved her driving as well). With her eyes wide open, she conversed with God. Each day she released her frustrations and grew stronger in her new role as a single parent. She had discovered a new tool to help her, but as long as she was a parent, she would experience times of tension.

Jesus' prayer removed His tension *at the moment* so that He was steeled to go on toward the cross. But there would be more tension, as we will see in the next two chapters.

Some kinds of tension can be removed once and for all with prayer, especially the kind of prayer we discussed in the solitude section; but there is also tension that is ongoing with God's will. This kind of tension can be relieved, but we can't expect it not to return. Being a committed Christian is to be involved in spiritual warfare (Ephesians 6:10–13). As long as we have two opposing forces battling for our allegiance, we will experience tension. We should not condemn ourselves for experiencing it; rather, we should acknowledge and face it honestly by praying, "Now my heart is troubled, and what shall I say? 'Father, save me from this hour'? No, this is what being a Christian is all about. Father, glorify your name!"

making the
CONNECTION

How will knowing that Jesus experienced mental and emotional strain help me pray?

What is one thing I need to remember when I think I don't have time to pray or when I don't know what to pray?

Notes

1. The sequencing of events that led to Jesus' honest prayer is based on A. T. Robertson's *A Harmony of the Gospels for Students of the Life of Christ* (New York: Harper, 1922, 1950).

2. Luke–John, *The Broadman Bible Commentary* (Nashville: Broadman, 1970), 9:322.

3. Author's paraphrase of John 12:32.

the cup
of suffering

*"Abba, Father," he said, "everything is possible for you. Take this cup
from me. Yet not what I will, but what you will."*
—Mark 14:36

Jesus' honest admission of a troubled heart occurred on
Monday. By late Thursday evening, the struggle over
doing God's will was back. Distress and anguish came
over Him (Mark 14:33), and "he began to be sorrowful and troubled" (Matthew 26:37). How can this be? If
God answered Jesus' prayer on Monday, giving Him the
strength and determination to proceed towards the
cross, why is He troubled again? To answer that question requires a look at prayer and a look at Jesus.

a Look at prayer

Sometimes prayer ends a struggle once and for all.
We pour out our feelings, lay our needs before the Lord,
and He responds. Peace enters our heart, and we feel

strengthened to go on, confident God will give us everything we need to deal with our particular situation.

But for some things we pray about, the struggle may be ongoing. Through prayer, we get relief; but if the circumstances we are dealing with don't change and the tension persists, and we may find ourselves praying about the same issues.

For example, you are diagnosed with a serious illness, with a high possibility of its being terminal. You are angry, frightened, grieved. You express your feelings to God, holding nothing back. Finally you accept the possibility of death, and God's peace fills your heart. You tell your friends, "I'm ready to go." You are surprised then when a week later you wake in the night gasping for breath and terrified of dying.

Or, you are called to the ministry. You fight it for months, reluctant to give up your lifestyle and make the necessary sacrifices. You tell God how you feel; you remind Him that He has singled out the wrong person. But the call persists, and through a long prayer vigil filled with sweat and tears, you finally surrender. Peace fills your soul and sustains you through your training, but when you actually become pastor of a church, you start doubting your call. You are overwhelmed with people's problems and concerns. Your serving becomes strained; your sermons are lifeless. You wonder, *Did I really hear God right? Maybe I shouldn't be in the ministry.* You pray, "God, I want out."

Perhaps it's not your health or your service, but a relationship. You might have been so in sync with your spouse when you married that you were shocked the first time you had a major disagreement. Your disappointment was keen, and you prayed it out, asking God to help you forgive your spouse, and He did. The inner serenity and calmness was so sweet you thought, *We've learned a good lesson here; now we can keep this kind of thing from ever happening again.* If someone who had been married for a long time were hearing your thoughts, at this point he or she would chuckle and say, "How naive can you be!" Life changes, we change, and circumstances change, so some struggles we experience will need prayer, time and time again. A one-time prayer, no matter how satisfying the answer, may not see us through forever.

That Jesus' struggle with God's will was back on Thursday night did not mean that Jesus' prayer on Monday was ineffective or that God's answer wasn't sufficient. It was the nature of the struggle He was experiencing that led to a return of His distress.

a Look at his struggle

God had given Jesus a task to complete, a mission to accomplish. As Jesus stated in His own words, "For the Son of Man came to seek and to save" (Luke 19:10). As we mentioned in chapter 2, Jesus' compliance wasn't automatic, as if He were a robot. If that were the case, Satan wouldn't have bothered to tempt Him.

Bottom line, the task was about Jesus' drawing people to God and giving His life as a ransom for the sins of men and women, but it went beyond that. It meant living a life that would reveal God's heart, so it was important to be compassionate and kind. It meant seeing to it that followers were trained so that the story of what God was doing would live on after Jesus was no longer on earth.

A time element was attached to the completing of His mission. Whenever a time element is involved it adds to the tension. Think of how tense the end of a college semester is compared to the beginning. Think of how the stress builds getting ready for a major celebration such as a wedding. Everyone knows it is going to happen on a certain date, but still the tension builds. The closer Jesus got to the cross—to when His mission would be completed—the greater the intensity of what He was experiencing. His enemies continued to oppose Him, Satan never ceased trying to deflect Him from His ministry, people continued to press close to Him with needs and questions, and His disciples needed more training.

All the while, death, necessary to completing His mission, was staring Him in the face. If Jesus fully entered the human situation, He would have resisted death as any mentally healthy person would. As the moment for His death drew near, He had a heightened awareness of and appreciation for life and naturally resisted dying, especially the kind of death He would experience. He would have to endure rejection and public execution. He would have to surrender Himself to the dreadful shame of a criminal's death, to abuse, and to excruciating pain. And worse, He would have to become the scapegoat, the sacrificial lamb who would bear the world's sins, and He felt the awful weight bearing down on Him.

When the stress of doing God's will wrapped itself around Him on Monday, His honest, brief confession brought relief, enabling Him to carry on, but there was no change in the external circumstances. If anything, His enemies were more vehement in their opposition and the devil was more earnest in his efforts. All the while the clock was ticking. There was so much to say and do. No wonder He needed to pray again by Thursday night; only this time He wanted a private place to pray. Jesus headed for the Mount of Olives, a place where He was accustomed to retreating (Luke 22:39).

IN THE GARDEN

Jesus took His disciples with Him. Maybe it was the natural thing to do because they had been together all evening. They had eaten the Passover meal together and Jesus had spent the remainder of the evening comforting and preparing them (John 14–16) for the future. Or perhaps He took them with Him to insulate Him from His enemies and curiosity seekers so that He could concentrate on praying. Or maybe He wanted their support. As we noted in chapter 6, one of the reasons Jesus chose the Twelve was that they might be with Him (Mark 3:14), and on this night, He wanted them to share His vigil, not that they could do anything, but just that they might be there offering a comforting presence.

He left eight of the apostles at the garden gate. (Judas had left the group during the Passover meal.) He said to them, "Sit here while I pray" (Mark 14:32).

Jesus took Peter, James, and John with Him deeper into the garden. At this point, the Bible says Jesus "*began* to be deeply distressed and troubled" (v. 33, italics added). Curtis C. Mitchell, who did a thorough study of this prayer, reported, "The word *began* indicates the commencement of a new level of sorrow more severe in degree than our Lord had ever experienced before!"[1]

Jesus confessed His feelings to Peter, James, and John. "He said to them, 'My soul is overwhelmed with sorrow to the point of death'" (Matthew 26:38). *Today's English Version* translates this statement as "The sorrow in my heart is so great that it almost crushes me." The *New American Standard Bible* says, "My soul is deeply grieved, to the point of death."

Why this new level of sorrow when the struggle is basically the same as it was? Here are three possible explanations.

Once the disciples' training was complete, Jesus could let His emotions surface. One of Jesus' primary concerns was training the disciples and preparing them for the future. On Tuesday He spent the afternoon teaching them about His second coming and about the forthcoming destruction of Jerusalem. On Thursday evening, He comforted them and prepared them for the future (John 14–16). Then, as if the last details were taken care of, He prayed for them, giving them and their future to God (John 17). Once they had been committed to God, Jesus could let His emotions about His struggle surface.

What responsible adult hasn't experienced this kind of thing? Even when you are struggling on the inside, your work goes on and obligations still must be met. You go on waiting for a time and place to deal with your emotions. Sometimes you can pray quick, honest prayers, such as Jesus did on Monday, but feelings still remain below the surface, waiting to be dealt with.

I remember once when my husband and I were jolted by a job loss right before we were to fly to a conference center in another state to be workshop leaders. Because I had to make sure the children were taken care of, clothes were packed, speeches finished, I couldn't allow myself to think about what happened. When we arrived at the conference center, we were busy greeting people, getting instructions, and attending the opening ceremony. Through it all, I was applying "God, help me" Band-Aid prayers, but that night when the lights were out, I let the fear, the anxiety, the shock surface, and it was awful. I felt as if I were wrestling with the devil himself. When you hold feelings back—as we often must—their surfacing can be very painful.

Jesus was starkly reminded of His death. Perhaps as Jesus and the Eleven crossed the brook of Kidron (see John 18:1), He was reminded of His coming death by the color of the water, and grief suddenly overwhelmed Him. Grief has a way of coming on unexpectedly. You think you are doing fine dealing with loss when something unexpected will trigger a wave of grief that washes over you. The color of the water in the Kidron was red from the blood of the lambs slain upon the altar for the Passover. The number of lambs slain was great, probably over two hundred thousand. From the altar where the lambs were slain, a channel ran down to the brook Kidron. Through that channel the blood of the Passover lambs drained away. As Jesus crossed the brook, the reality of His own blood being shed and the pain that would go with it might have come upon Him in full force and exceeded what He had expected.[2]

The devil pulled out all of the stops. Satan had tempted Jesus time and again to set up a kingdom that did not involve the cross. His ministry began with that temptation (Mark 1:12–13). What happened in the garden was a renewal of that temptation; only now, with the cross so near, Satan pulled out all the stops.

If you find this possibility hard to believe, remember that Jesus experienced temptation like we never have or will. The fact that Jesus was without sin means that He knew depths and assaults of temptation we will never know. We fall to temptation long before Satan has put out the whole of His power. Jesus' battle with temptation wasn't easier because He was sinless; it was immeasurably harder.

Regardless of the explanation, the Bible is clear about Jesus' being deeply distressed, troubled, and overwhelmed with sorrow. "Some experts feel it was the very force of His emotions that drove Him"[3] to pray. He moved beyond James, John, and Peter; "fell with his face to the ground" (Matthew 26:39); and prayed that if possible He might not have to go through the suffering. He prayed for a way out. "Abba, Father," he said, "everything is possible for you. Take this cup from me" (Mark 14:36). Wasn't this request a waste of time? He couldn't escape the cross, could He?

the complexity of his struggle

There is the possibility that Jesus' prayer for an escape was an emotional release, expressing the agony of His soul, and nothing more. Sometimes a cry like that will help when we are up against something we can't change.

On the other hand, escape routes were open to Jesus. If they weren't, that would have made a mockery of His willingly choosing to die for us (John 10:17–18).

- In the darkness of the night, He could have slipped out of Jerusalem.
- He could have compromised with the religious leaders and diluted their hostility.
- He could have called on legions of angels to come to His defense (Matthew 26:51–54).

At the same time—and this is what makes His struggle so complex—Jesus wanted to do what God wanted. "Yet not as I will, but as you will" (Matthew 26:39). Jesus knew the cross was essential to the plan, purpose, and design of God, whom He wanted to please. If He wanted to be the obedient Son, escape was not possible.

The tension between wanting an escape and wanting to please God was real and intense, as His praying revealed.

HONEST, emotional PRAYING

Jesus' praying in Gethsemane was no short, pithy praying, even though the Bible records Him as saying the same thing three times. If it had been, the disciples would not have had time to fall asleep, and they did. After Jesus prayed, asking for a way out but also stating He wanted to do God's will, He returned to the disciples and found them sleeping. "'Could you men not keep watch with me for one hour?' he asked Peter. 'Watch and pray so that you will not fall into temptation. The spirit is willing, but the body is weak'" (Matthew 26:40–41).

Neither would He have needed an angel to appear and strengthen Him (Luke 22:43). "Being in an agony he prayed more earnestly" (Luke 22:44 KJV). According to Mitchell, the origin of the word translated "agony" (or "anguish" in the NIV) "is taken from the struggle and pain of an athletic contest. The full expression, 'being in an agony' (Luke 22:44 KJV), conveys the idea of growing intensity. Christ had progressed in struggle from the first prayer into an even more intensive combat"[4] as He continued to pray.

As if the struggle of an athletic contest is not enough to describe what Jesus was going through, Luke says "his sweat was as . . . great drops of blood falling down to the ground" (22:44 KJV). We usually think of sweat as a phenomenon associated with physical work. Jesus must have been experiencing incredible agony for His sweat to turn to blood during a time of prayer. Under great emotional stress, tiny capillaries in the sweat glands can break, mixing the blood and the sweat. This process alone is enough to produce weakness and possible shock.

As Jesus emotionally and honestly admitted His struggle to God, He felt no need for cover-up or pretense. He was as open with God as a child is who has never been taught, "You shouldn't feel that way." Jesus called God *Abba*, which was the Aramaic (Jesus' native tongue) address of a small child to his father. It was an everyday word, a homey family word. Jesus spoke with God as a child speaks with his loving father, simply, intimately, securely, and openly.

If Jesus, who knew the Father intimately, offered His prayer in this manner, then we should feel free to do likewise. There is no need to hide our emotions from God, since He is aware of their existence even before we are (Matthew 6:8). The Bible says that "all things are naked and opened unto the eyes of him with whom we have to do" (Hebrews 4:13 KJV), so we do not need to conceal anything from God. With childlike trust, we may bare our hearts before Him, tell Him how we feel, and even ask for an escape.

It is not only OK for us to be honest about our feelings as we pray, it is important that we are. One of the reasons we pray is to offer God a channel of receptivity in which He can respond to us. Unexpressed emotions clog up that channel. Honest praying moves them out so that God can come in and do a work of grace in us as He did with Jesus.

the change in Jesus

When Jesus returned to His disciples, He said, "Look, the hour is near, and the Son of Man is betrayed into the hands of sinners. Rise, let us go! Here comes my betrayer!" (Matthew 26:45–46).

Judas and a large crowd armed with swords and clubs arrived to arrest Him. They carried lamps and torches as if they might have to search among the trees and in the hillside nooks and crannies to find Jesus. "They must have assumed that He would hide. So far from hiding, when they arrived, Jesus stepped out. 'Who are you looking for?' He demanded. 'Jesus of Nazareth,' they said. Back came the answer: 'I am He.' The man they had thought they would have to search for as He skulked in the trees and the caves was standing before them with a glorious, reckless defiance."[5] He was ready to drink the cup the Father had given Him (see John 18:11).

Power radiated from Jesus as He continued toward the cross with confidence and determination. Everything about

Him and what He did during the early morning hours of Friday as He was shuffled from one authority to the next indicated He was in control. In the midst of turbulence, He was tranquil because He had prayed honestly. Jesus, who entered the garden distressed, left it in strength to accomplish God's will. The cup, which was not removed, became the cup that was poured out for the redemption of mankind.

making the
CONNECTION

Was Jesus' struggle a spiritual one or an emotional one?

What does the name I call God reveal about my relationship with Him?

Notes

1. Curtis C. Mitchell, *Praying Jesus' Way* (Old Tappan, N.J.: Revell, 1977), 59.

2. William Barclay, *The Gospel of John,* 3d ed., vol. 2, The Daily Study Bible (Edinburgh: Saint Andrew, 1964), 259.

3. Mitchell, *Praying Jesus' Way*, 61.

4. Ibid., 62–63.

5. William Barclay, *The Gospel of John,* vol. 2, 261.

the cry
of utter
Loneliness

At the sixth hour darkness came over the whole land until the ninth hour. And at the ninth hour Jesus cried out in a loud voice, "Eloi, Eloi, lama sabachthani?"—which means, "My God, my God, why have you forsaken me?"

—Mark 15:33-34

Once Jesus was arrested late Thursday night, so-called trials were hastily conducted, and by nine o'clock Friday morning, Jesus was hanging on the cross. Two thieves were crucified along with Him. At His feet, Roman soldiers gambled for His garments. Curious spectators gathered. They hurled insults at Jesus and mocked Him. "So! You who are going to destroy the temple and build it in three days, come down from the cross and save yourself!" (Mark 15:29–30).

Mingling among the spectators, the chief priests and the scribes talked contemptuously among themselves: "He saved others, but he can't save himself! Let this Christ, this King of Israel, come down now from the cross, that we may see and believe" (Mark 15:31–32).

The soldiers also participated in the jeering. They

offered Jesus some of their sour wine, and said, "If you are the king of the Jews, save yourself" (Luke 23:37).

One of the thieves also railed against Jesus. "Aren't you the Christ? Save yourself and us!" (Luke 23:39).

The mocking and jeering ceased at noon when a strange darkness fell like a heavy curtain over the earth. Silence reigned as a feeling of awe and horror descended on everyone. For three ominous hours, Jesus hung on the cross in darkness. As the agonies of the crucifixion deepened, He cried out in a loud voice. The cry was so awful that it seared itself in the memory of Matthew and Mark as it was said in Aramaic, *"Eloi, Eloi, lama sabachthani."* It means, "My God, My God, why have you forsaken Me?"

Aramaic was Jesus' native tongue, and not everyone present understood it, so there was some confusion. Some people thought He was calling Elijah to rescue Him. Some understood Him to say "Eloi, Eloi"; others thought He said, "Eli, Eli." Some thought He wanted something to drink (Matthew 21:47–49; Mark 15:35–36).

The prayer confuses us, too, but for different reasons. It is not the Aramaic but the "forsaken" aspect that puzzles us. This word gives the impression that Jesus felt God was not present in the sense in which He had always been. How could this be when the precious Son was pleasing the Father by laying down His life for the redemption of the human race? It looks as though this would be a time of closeness instead of blocked fellowship. And even more disturbing, if Jesus felt forsaken, does that mean He really was forsaken?

The way Jesus communicated with God at this moment is such a contrast to the way we have seen Him pray earlier. That "Abba, Father" closeness we talked about in the last chapter is missing. The "Father," "O Righteous Father," and "Holy Father" that He prayed in His Thursday evening prayer for the disciples is absent. Instead, it is "My God, My God." At no other time does He address God in this manner. This is clearly a moment like no other in His life. Why is it different?

Several factors may be involved.

bearer of sins

Up to this moment Jesus had gone through every experience of life except one: being separated from God because of sin. Jesus had taken this life of ours upon Himself. He had done our work and faced our temptations and borne our trials. He had suffered all that life could bring to Him. He had known the failure of friends, the hatred of foes, the malice of enemies, but He had never known the consequence of sin.

Sin separates us from God. It puts up between God and us a barrier that is like an unscalable wall. Jesus had never experienced that because He was without sin. When Jesus hung on the cross, identifying Himself with the sin of humanity (2 Corinthians 5:21), He felt the weight of the burden and what it was to be separated from God by sin. This experience must have been agonizing for Him, because He had never known what it was to be separated from God. His fellowship with God, which had always sustained Him, was not present now. As He drank the cup of the wrath of God against sin, He felt passing over Him the awful loneliness of a soul bereft of God. Compounding this loneliness was lack of support from those around Him and those who knew Him.

Lack of support

In his book *The Lord's Prayers*, Elton Trueblood wrote that the loneliness must have been almost unbearable for Jesus. It is true that we often count on the support of fellow believers to help us through difficult times. We credit their support as God's doing—His way of letting us know He is with us. When we don't have that kind of support, loneliness engulfs us. Jesus had little support at the cross. Trueblood said, "The crowd, instead of being moved to compassion by His suffering, were either idly curious or openly glad that He was in torment.

Instead of compassion which He needed at this point, He received ridicule."[1]

Jesus was scoffed by the soldiers and the crowd. As the executioners claimed His clothing as their right, He must have thought of another person, a psalmist, who felt besieged and forsaken. The psalmist had said, "They divide my garments among them and cast lots for my clothing" (Psalm 22:18). As chief priests, scribes, and elders scoffed and mocked Him, Jesus recalled the psalmist's words, "All who see me mock me; they hurl insults, shaking their heads: He trusts in the LORD; let the LORD rescue him" (vv. 7–8).

Some women followers stood at a distance, but "where were the Twelve to whom He had given His closest attention? Where were the members of the innermost circle, once gathered for prayer on the Mountain of Transfiguration?"[2]

> The most acute kind of loneliness is not caused by the absence of other persons. It is the aloneness that engulfs us when we are unable to sense that others are sharing, caring, supporting, or identifying with us in a time of great need. To be in the midst of people and not be able to sense that others know, or care to know, what is happening inside you—that is a loneliness which separates and isolates.[3]

The awful loneliness Jesus was experiencing must have been exacerbated by what He was physically suffering.

THE PAIN OF THE CROSS

Long iron nails were driven between the bones of Jesus' wrists into the wood crossbar. The nails usually tore through the median nerve. This would have created an unending trail of fire up His arms, augmenting the pain from the long spike through His ankles. The rigidity of His position caused muscle cramps. Dehydration created intense thirst.

Jesus was already so weak from the whipping He received preceding the Crucifixion that the Roman soldiers had to tap

Simon of Cyrene to carry His cross (Mark 15:21; Luke 23:26). Now, nailed to the cross, He couldn't even swipe at the gnats and flies that swarmed around the dried blood on His head and back. He couldn't wipe the sweat from His forehead.

Excruciating pain for hours at a time can make a person feel abandoned by God, as many cancer patients or burn victims will tell you. To me, it takes nothing away from Jesus' humanity or His divinity if His cry of abandonment had something to do with the physical torture of the Crucifixion. A human body was suffering as well as a human soul. If His pain contributed to His feeling forsaken by God, that makes His sacrifice (and love) for me all the greater.

The Gospel writers carefully note the time element—three long hours of darkness—as if during this time the spiritual, emotional, and physical factors increased in intensity to an agony that exceeded that of Gethsemane. Feeling utterly alone, Jesus cried out with the words of the psalmist He had been thinking about, "My God, my God, why have you forsaken me?"[4]

> He sensed like the psalmist before him, that he was all alone. God had left him comfortless. Although he was committed to obeying God's will and suffering death by way of the cross, he could not help but express his agony. There is no need to assume that Jesus had foreknown all that he was now experiencing. It is here more than anywhere else that the cost of his fulfilling the will of the Father becomes clear.[5]

Fortunately, this kind of experience is not the norm for life. It wasn't for Jesus, and it isn't for us. But, in the human experience, for some of us there come times when we feel God and everyone else has forgotten us. That is what happened to Jesus. In the Garden of Gethsemane, Jesus knew that He had to go on, because to go on was God's will, and He struggled to accept that. Here we see Jesus doing God's will and yet feeling forsaken by Him and by others. Even in the midst of doing right, we can feel forsaken, but does this mean we are forsaken?

facts vs. feeLINGS

The Bible promises us that God will never leave us or forsake us (Deuteronomy 31:6; Joshua 1:5; Hebrews 13:5). That's true even though we sometimes *feel* forsaken. While Jesus felt forsaken, events around the cross reveal that God did not abandon Him.

The supernatural darkness. What nature did at this time shows us God's heart. Jesus' death was so terrible that the sky was unnaturally darkened, as if nature could not bear to look. The darkness was not due to an eclipse because it was the time of the full moon of Passover week. The "simplest explanation is that it was a supernatural manifestation in nature . . . in sympathy with the crucial experience through which nature's Maker was passing during those three hours."[6]

Death came in a short time. Because no major organs were affected, crucifixion was usually a slow death. It sometimes took days. Jesus died in six hours. It was as if God were saying, "The cross may be necessary, but I'll not have You suffer any longer than is necessary."

The splitting of the veil in the temple. God responded as a Jewish father would at the death of his son.[7] When Jacob saw the multicolored coat of his beloved Joseph drenched in blood, he rent his garment as an expression of deepest sorrow. When Job got the shocking news of the death of his children, he tore his clothes as a symbol of his anguish.

"When Jesus bowed His head and died, God rent the veil from top to bottom, symbolically exposing His heart of sorrow—His suffering love."[8]

"By that vivid gesture, God indicated to Jesus' followers that He had personally been close by during the whole, terrible ordeal. God is not distant and unfeeling. He did not coldly send His Son to a cross."[9]

God responded to Jesus' prayer. After Jesus' prayer of abandonment, God strengthened Him and their closeness returned.

Jesus gave a victorious shout (Matthew 27:50; Mark 15:37; Luke 23:46): "It is finished!" (John 19:30 NASB). In the Greek, that would have been one word: "Finished!" It was the shout of a man who had completed the task, a man who had won through the struggle, a man who had come out of darkness into light. Jesus died with the cry of triumph on His lips, His task accomplished, His work completed, His victory won. His shout was "not the weakened utterance of one dying from physical exhaustion, but of a Conqueror in the full flush of strength and victory."[10]

After this shout, Jesus prayed a prayer that shows that fellowship was restored. Again He used the words of a psalmist, "Into your hands I commit my spirit" (Psalm 31–5; Luke 23:46). Jews often used this sentence as a prayer, adding the word *Father* to it. Jewish mothers taught their children to say this prayer when they lay down to sleep at night. Perhaps Mary had taught the prayer to Jesus. When He was dying, Jesus prayed the prayer He had probably prayed many times as a little boy.

Following the prayer, Jesus bowed His head and died. The Gospel writer John said that Jesus bowed His head and gave up His spirit. "The word that John [used] is the word, which might be used for settling back upon a pillow. For Jesus the strife was over and the battle was won."[11] So there came to Jesus the peace after His long battle, rest after His earnest work, and contentment knowing He had completed His task. With the sure and restful sigh of a tired child, He died, confident of His Father's care and no longer feeling forsaken.

Taken together, these events tell us that God did not forsake Jesus, and this should console us during times when we feel forsaken and alone. The fact is we are not abandoned; how do we translate that fact into feeling? Instead of facts *versus* feelings, how do we make facts *equal* feelings? The same way Jesus did: through honest praying.

daring to ask "why?"

"[Jesus] did not for one minute fail in obedience, yet he

151

dared to ask "Why?" He did not curse God like his neighbor on the cross. But he questioned him."[12] And His example gives us permission to ask "Why?" when we are sincerely baffled by what we are experiencing. Honest praying opens the channel of communication we have with God, so He can respond as these three illustrations reveal.

A hurting father. After Lloyd Preston Terrell's oldest son, Lloyd Jr., and some college friends were severely injured in an automobile accident, all kinds of questions surfaced: "Oh, God, why did this happen to our son and his friends? Will Lloyd and his friends live? If he lives, will he be able to walk and live a normal life?"[13]

Terrell said that Satan tried to answer the questions by tempting him to doubt God's grace, love, and healing power—tempting him to doubt the facts. Terrell and his wife, though, did some honest praying. "We got real with Him. We told Him all about our troubles, fears, and doubts. We cried out to the Lord to help Lloyd and his friends. Somewhere in the *honesty* of those prayers, angels ministered to our souls. God heard us and gave us peace in turmoil. He did not remove our suffering, but He gave us the grace to face each day."[14]

A perplexed Christian. In his book *Surprised by Children,* Harold Myra tells about how his parents cared for several foster children who came from terrible circumstances. One of them, Ritchie, was with his foster parents for seven years and made a faith commitment before being returned to his mother. A few years later, Ritchie murdered Mrs. Prossler, a neighbor to Myra's parents.

Myra was baffled by this. His mother had reached out to Ritchie, nurtured him, introduced him to Christ's love, and he had been responding before being taken away. Myra wondered, "How could [he] be pulled away into disruption, temptation, devastation?"[15]

His mind was in turmoil. He burst out with his complaint against God. Seeing Ritchie as trapped and doomed, Myra tearfully said, "How could you do this? . . . Lord, how can you run your world with such capricious horror?"

Sometimes we wonder if we dare be honest with God, but Myra said that His "response was crystal clear: 'I'm not upset by your prayers.' On the contrary, it was as if God had been waiting for me to look evil full in the face and confront him.

"God seemed to say, 'How do you think I feel about Ritchie? About Mrs. Prossler? Haven't I wept over them? Haven't I sent my Son to die for them?'

"This flowed into me as a personal, forceful connection with God. I sensed that he was drawing me into his perspective, that he was calling me almost as a colleague to join forces in extending his love, to intercede for others in their helplessness— and that he was indeed in charge, transcending all tragedies."[16]

A weary cancer patient. In *Good Housekeeping* magazine, Joni Rodgers described her bout with an aggressive cancer of the lymphatic system. As she endured the cycles of chemo-therapy, she observed how the illness was affecting those she loved. One day in an emotional outburst, she sobbed a prayer. "I never once asked you *why me,* but why my family? My parents do not deserve to be put through this! My children do not deserve to witness this! My husband does not deserve to share in this! You've made me a source of pain to everyone I care about! *Do you even see what's going on?*"[17]

There was no thunderclap, no special epiphany that happened in response to her honest prayer, but in the quiet that followed her fury, it occurred to her that you don't get angry at someone who isn't there, and that was reassuring. He was present; He was close; He had not forsaken her.

If you will notice, dramatic answers did not occur in any of these instances. Terrell's son still had to recover, Ritchie was still a murderer, and Joni still had cancer. What changed were feelings. After their honest praying, the people no longer felt abandoned by God. Like the psalmist Jesus quoted, they could conclude, "For he has not despised or disdained the suffering of the afflicted one; he has not hidden his face from him but has listened to his cry for help" (Psalm 22:24). Honest praying will change your feelings to match the facts.

| making the |
| CONNECTION |

How is Jesus' cry of abandonment both awful and consoling?

What is one way I can express my feelings of abandonment?

Notes

1. Elton Trueblood, *The Lord's Prayers* (New York: Harper & Row, 1965), 121–22.
2. Ibid., 122.
3. Millard Osborne, "The Word of Loneliness," *The Way of the Cross and Resurrection,* edited by John M. Drescher (Scottdale, Pa.: Herald, 1978), 157.
4. See Psalm 22:1.
5. Robert H. Stein, *Jesus the Messiah: A Survey of the Life of Christ* (Downers Grove, Ill.: InterVarsity, 1996), 251.
6. J. W. Shepard, *The Christ of the Gospels: An Exegetical Study* (Grand Rapids: Eerdmans, 1956), 601.
7. Randal Earl Denny, *In the Shadow of the Cross* (Kansas City, Mo.: Beacon Hill, 1995), 111.
8. Ibid.
9. Ibid.
10. Shepard, *The Christ of the Gospels,* 603.
11. William Barclay, *The Gospel of John,* 3d., vol. 2, The Daily Study Bible (Edinburgh: Saint Andrew, 1964), 301.
12. Margaret Magdalen, *Jesus, Man of Prayer* (Downers Grove, Ill.: InterVarsity, 1987), 142.
13. Lloyd Preston Terrell, "The Emotional Prayers of Jesus," *Pray!* September–October 1999, 20.

14. Ibid.

15. Harold Myra, *Surprised by Children* (Grand Rapids: Zondervan, 2001), 41.

16. Ibid.

17. Joni Rodgers, "Bald in the Land of Big Hair," *Good Housekeeping,* March 2001, 171.

PART FOUR

INTERCESSION

the cost of intercession

Then Jesus looked up and said, "Father, I thank you that you have heard me. . . ."

When he had said this, Jesus called in a loud voice, "Lazarus, come out!" . . .

Therefore many of the Jews . . . put their faith in him. But some of them went to the Pharisees and told them what Jesus had done. . . .

So from that day on they plotted to take his life.

—John 11:41, 43, 45–46, 53

I once read about a minister in England who got word one evening that his closest friend in the ministry was critically ill. He was not expected to live through the night. Upon receiving this news, he went to his study and fell on his knees. He began to pray that this man's life might be spared. He acknowledged his affection for his friend and the sense of promise that he felt for his future. As he did this, from somewhere a voice spoke to him saying, "Just how serious are you about this one's life being spared? Would you be willing to relinquish half the years that you have left so that they might be added to his lifespan?"[1]

Something similar happened to Jesus near the end of His ministry—an incident that will begin our study of the final cornerstone of His prayer life. Jesus, though, wasn't asked to give half of the years He had left for a friend. He was asked to give His life.

THE REQUEST

At the time, Jesus and His disciples were in Perea. He had taken them there because the atmosphere in Jerusalem and Judea where He had been ministering had become hostile. In Perea, where people were more open-minded and less critical, Jesus could minister more freely. While there, word came to Him of the grave illness of His friend, Lazarus, the brother of Martha and Mary, who lived near Jerusalem, in Bethany of Judea. Via a messenger, the sisters said, "Lord, the one you love is sick" (John 11:3). The implied message was "Please come and do something."

"When he heard this, Jesus said, 'This sickness will not end in death. No, it is for God's glory so that God's Son may be glorified through it'" (v. 4).

When the messenger took Jesus' statement back to Mary and Martha, I'm sure they were encouraged and comforted— at least, by the first part of the message.[2] It was good news indeed that their brother's sickness would not end in death, but what did Jesus mean by the rest of the statement?

Jesus said that Lazarus' sickness had happened for God's glory and for His. Undoubtedly, in the cure of Lazarus, men and women would be able to see the glory of God in action. Recently, a friend told me about two phenomenal turnarounds in the illnesses of two women in her church. Both had mysterious illnesses and both were now remarkably recovered. Jan said, "I tell you this was nothing less than the power of God at work."

Mighty works glorify God, but there was more to Jesus' statement than that kind of glory. When Jesus talked of being glorified, He often meant the cross.

- In John 7:39, the Spirit had not yet come because Jesus was not yet *glorified,* that is, because Jesus had not yet died upon His cross.

- In John 12:16, the disciples remembered "these things" after Jesus had been *glorified,* that is, after He had died and risen again.

- When the Greeks came to Him, Jesus said, "The hour has come for the Son of Man to be *glorified"* (John 12:23, italics added). It was of the cross that He spoke, for He went right on, talking about the kernel of wheat which must fall into the ground and die (v. 24).

- After Judas left the supper in the Upper Room to betray Jesus, He said, "Now is the Son of Man glorified and God is glorified in him" (John 13:31). The despicable act of betrayal was done; the cross was a certainty.

"Jesus regarded the Cross both as His supreme glory and as the way to glory. So, when Jesus said that the cure of Lazarus would glorify Him, He was showing that He knew perfectly well that to go to Bethany and to cure Lazarus was to take a step which would end in the Cross."[3] In other words, going back to the Bethany-Jerusalem area was going to be dangerous. Jesus knew it, and the disciples knew it.

BUT RABBI . . .

When Jesus said to the disciples, "Let us go back to Judea" (John 11:7), they were incredulous. "'But Rabbi,' they said, 'a short while ago the Jews tried to stone you, and yet you are going back there?'" (v. 8). To them, it was madness to return. His enemies were set upon destroying Him (8:59; 10:31). Only a short time earlier, He had narrowly escaped stoning (10:22–39). To return to Bethany, just outside of Jerusalem in Judea, was a sure way to encounter life-threatening danger.

Jesus responded with a proverb: "Are there not twelve hours

of daylight? A man who walks by day will not stumble, for he sees by this world's light. It is when he walks by night that he stumbles, for he has no light" (11:9–10).

Jesus thought of the whole of His mission as "my day" (8:56). Although it was the late afternoon of His "day," Jesus was saying that it was still light. He would, therefore, carry on; He would not falter nor stumble; He would go on.

Determined, Jesus said, "Let us go to Lazarus."

Thomas said to the disciples, "Let us also go, that we may die with him" (11:16). Thomas was convinced that going back where hostile eyes were searching for Jesus and hostile hearts were plotting His doom was nothing less than deliberate suicide.

BACK IN BETHANY

After they arrived in Bethany, Jesus talked with Martha and Mary and then went to Lazarus' tomb. He ordered the stone removed, and then He prayed. "Father, I thank you that you have heard me. I knew that you always hear me, but I said this for the benefit of the people standing here, that they may believe that you sent me" (John 11:41–42).

Then Jesus called in a loud voice, "Lazarus, come out!" (v. 43).

Lazarus came out of the tomb. "His hands and feet [were] wrapped with strips of linen, and a cloth around his face" (v. 44), but he came out! Lazarus was alive!

Many of the Jews who saw Lazarus come out of the tomb now believed in Jesus. But others were impressed in a different way. They were alarmed by such a colossal miracle and went to the religious leaders and told them what Jesus had done.

The religious leaders hurriedly assembled the Sanhedrin because they knew they had a problem on their hands. If Jesus were allowed to go on doing miracles like this, it was inevitable that the people would follow Him in even larger numbers. In a panic, they said, "What can we do? This man is doing many miracles. If we let him alone, all men will believe on him; and the Romans will come and take away both our place and our nation" (see 11:47–48).

Caiaphas, who was high priest that year, had no doubt about what to do. He spoke up, "Don't you know that it would be better for one person to die for the people than that the whole nation perish?" (see v. 50).

"It was a cold-blooded and deliberate incitement to murder; but it carried the day. And from that moment Christ was doomed. The smoldering hostility that had sporadically leaped up into a flame of open violence toward him"[4] now became a roaring blaze. In raising Lazarus from the dead, Jesus had committed the final and unpardonable act. For this they would kill Him. They didn't have a set plan yet, but they were determined to get Him. Praying for Lazarus cost Jesus, and it's possible that praying for others may cost us, too.

some costs

It was a sobering moment for the English minister (the one mentioned on the first page of this chapter) when he was asked if he would relinquish half the years he had left for his friend. He got up off his knees and broke out in a cold sweat. Up to that point, he had always thought of intercession as something God did exclusively, as if our prayer effort doesn't matter— but it does. We may not have to give our life as Jesus did (thankfully, that is not a biblical requirement for intercessors!), but prayer does require time, effort, and emotion.

Time. When I asked several prayers, "What does intercession cost you?" their primary answer was "Time." Sandie, a called and gifted intercessor, said, "God puts on me an 'anointing' to stay in prayer for hours at a time. I give up lots of activities—television, crafts, and sometimes family events—to make room for intercession."

It takes time to fully understand the need, weigh it, and think about how to pray, and it takes time to actually voice the prayer. Sometimes this may be a one-time event, but for many needs, the prayers may need to be continued for days and weeks, and in some cases, years.

This matter of needing time to intercede may explain why

Jesus delayed returning to Bethany. Jesus was always anxious to help, and He loved Mary, Martha, and Lazarus (11:5). Surely, He wouldn't want to keep them waiting at a time when they were deeply troubled, and yet He did. He stayed where He was two days before leaving for Bethany. At Lazarus' tomb, when Jesus prayed, He mentioned that God had heard Him, implying that the intercession for Lazarus had already taken place. When did He pray? Could it have been during that two-day delay? Between verses 6 and 7?

Verse 6 of John 11 says, "Yet when he heard that Lazarus was sick, he stayed where he was two more days." The first word of verse 7 is "Then," as if something significant had happened in those two days. It was at that time when He decisively said to the disciples, "Let us go back to Judea" (v. 7). During those two days Jesus wasn't forgetting His friends at Bethany nor ignoring their sorrow; He was wrestling in prayer on their behalf.

Effort. Wrestling is an apt description of intercessory prayer because spiritual, emotional, and physical energy are involved. Mary Rose, an intercessor for more than twenty years, said, "It expends spiritual energy to intercede and pray for others, and if I am not faithful to refresh myself in the Lord, the 'giving out' can become a burden."

Sometimes we have to expend so much effort because of the seriousness of the need, because the situation is complicated, or because spiritual warfare is involved. Sandie said, "When you start interceding for people, you are literally on the front lines. This sounds wild, I know, but the Lord has even brought me head-to-head with witches on different occasions, and it really is war. It wears you out physically and emotionally."

The unusualness and difficulty of Lazarus' case may be why Jesus needed time to pray even when He knew what the outcome would be.

How Jesus healed varied. Frequently, healing was with a word of authority or a touch, but prayer was seldom part of the action. An exception to this was the healing of a deaf and mute man (Mark 7:31–35). Jesus took him apart from the crowd, put

His fingers in the man's ears, spat, and touched the man's tongue. Then Jesus looked up to heaven (indicating prayer), gave a deep groan, and said to the man, "Open up!"

This doesn't mean prayer wasn't important to Jesus' healing ministry. After He healed the boy with the unclean spirit, something His disciples were unable to do, they asked, "Why couldn't we drive out the evil spirit?" "He replied, 'This kind can come out only by prayer'" (Mark 9:29).

Lazarus' case was different from any Jesus had responded to before. On two other occasions He had brought dead people back to life, but they had been dead only a short time. The twelve-year-old girl, the daughter of Jairus, was still on her deathbed (Mark 5:35–42). The dead son of the widow of Nain was being carried to the burial site (Luke 7:11–16).

Even if Jesus had left right away for Martha's house, Lazarus would still have been dead longer than these other two cases. Perhaps the very difficulty of this case required earnest intercession over two days.

Emotion. Chuck, who describes himself as "an intercessor by choice and discipline, not by giftedness," says that interceding for others costs him not only time but heart effort. He said, "What I mean by 'heart effort' is the personal burden I feel for others when I pray for them, and how my praying for them always drives me to personally stay in touch with them and follow up on their situations. When I pray for people, I'm driven to care about them . . . and caring takes effort!"

To be touched by needs that prompt us to pray for others involves an emotional cost. When Jesus prayed for the deaf mute, He heaved a deep sigh (Mark 7:34). When He healed the widow's son, His heart went out to her (Luke 7:13). Jesus was "deeply moved in spirit and troubled" (John 11:33) when He saw Mary and some of the mourners weeping. He wept with them (see v. 35) and was deeply moved when He arrived at the tomb (see v. 38).

Sandie described this emotional involvement as a "spirit of travail." She said, "It comes over me at unexpected times, and consequently, I've been embarrassed because some people don't understand when I start to weep for someone and have to excuse myself to go pray."

I'll admit I resist interceding for others because I'm a cost-counter. I'm often reluctant to spend the time and effort necessary to intercede, and I resist carrying the emotional burden that goes along with it. If you are like me, then you may be wondering, *Why bother? If intercession costs, then why do it? Why keep at it when it costs time, effort, and emotion?*

REASONS WE INTERCEDE

Unlike me, the intercessors I talked with tended to minimize the costs. Sandie was even hesitant to talk about costs. She said, "It is going to sound like I'm whining, and nothing is farther from the truth. The costs can't even begin to compare with the rewards."

Mary Rose admitted, "Yes, there is cost in investing time, energy, emotion, concern, and hope into prayer for people. But, oh, the returns that are reaped when you see fruit come forth in their lives."

Chuck put it a little more succinctly. He said the main reason he prayed for others is "Because God moves." He has seen answers to his prayers.

Susan was practical in her answer. "I am motivated by a desire to do what I can. Often that is prayer and nothing else. When I have faithfully prayed for a person or a need, I consider that a contribution to the solution and know that I have done what I can."

David, a contemplative prayer, said, "I want to be united with God in love. The great invitation of life in God is to love as God loves. To enter into the life of God includes in some way entering a life of intercession."

My motive is not as noble as David's. I intercede because I am haunted by Jesus' example. If I want a prayer life like Jesus', then praying for others is not an option. If intercession was indispensable to His prayer life, it should be indispensable to mine as well.

166

Mary Rose reminded me that the cost in *not* interceding is greater than the cost of intercession. She said, "The times that I have chosen to do my own thing and not obey His gentle, quiet leading has cost me peace, fulfillment, joy, and the other wonderful blessings of obedience."

I know what she means. In those times when I am tempted to let intercession slide, I notice my overall faith being affected. Without the cornerstone of intercession, my faith's vitality diminishes.

When Jesus explained to the disciples that they were returning to Bethany because Lazarus had died, He said that seeing His power to give life would give them new reason to believe; it would lead to a fuller, deeper faith (John 11:15).

Intercessory prayer can lead to a fuller, deeper faith. As Sandie said, "My intercession has led me to some remarkable discoveries and spiritual gifts that I wouldn't have wanted to miss. God has graciously given me spiritual eyes to see my purpose, and I long to fulfill that purpose. Being in His presence is joy unspeakable."

Mary Rose, who likened intercessory prayer to investing in others, praised the dividends as she grew closer to God. "What a boost and an encouragement to press in for more of God for myself when I see dear people walking in a blessing that I had the privilege of praying for!"

With so many possible dividends of intercession, are you open to investing?

the costs vs. the rewards

Jesus, with open eyes, paid the cost—accepted the cross—to help His friend Lazarus. He knew going to Jerusalem would be dangerous, yet He went.

The English minister who heard the voice ask, "Just how serious are you about this one's life being spared? Would you be willing to relinquish half the years that you have left?" began to think about his own life—his family, ministry, and the things he wanted to do. Then he thought about the life of his friend, his family, and ministry. For a long time he carefully set each of these realities over against the other and pondered their relative value. After a while, with clear resolve, he slipped back on his knees and said quietly: "Yes! I have considered the matter and the prolongation of the life of my friend is so precious to me that I hereby relinquish half of the years that I have remaining to me in his behalf."

The Englishman's friend survived, and Lazarus' life was restored to him. As Chuck would say, "God moved." Who knows what possibilities could occur when we are willing to pay the cost of intercession? As we study Jesus' acts of intercession, we have to ask ourselves, "Just how serious are we? Do we really want to pray as Jesus prayed?"

making the CONNECTION

Am I more conscious of the costs or the rewards of intercessory prayer?

What can I expect intercessory prayer to do for my faith?

Notes

1. I read this story in a sermon written by John R. Claypool, "Bearing One Another's Burdens," and preached at Northminster Baptist Church, Jackson, Mississippi, 10 June 1979.

2. J. W. Shepard, in *The Christ of the Gospels: An Exegetical Study* (Grand

Rapids: Eerdmans, 1956), 433, suggests the possibility of the messenger taking Jesus' words back to Mary and Martha. This would explain their distress when they greet Jesus on His arrival in Bethany ("If you had been here, my brother would not have died") and Jesus' question to Martha ("Did I not tell you that if you believed, you would see the glory of God?" [John 11:40]).

3. William Barclay, *The Gospel of John,* 3d. ed., vol. 2, The Daily Study Bible (Edinburgh: Saint Andrew, 1964), 94–95.

4. *The Interpreter's Bible* (Nashville: Abingdon, 1955), 8:651.

the power of intercession

"Simon, Simon, Satan has asked to sift you as wheat. But I have prayed for you, Simon, that your faith may not fail. And when you have turned back, strengthen your brothers."
—Luke 22:31–32

I once had some students in my college New Testament class who chose to portray the Passover meal—the Last Supper, we call it—for their class project. As I watched them enthusiastically gather props and make costumes, I looked forward to their presentation, certain that it was going to be well done. Well, the props and costumes were good, but they ate the meal in total silence except for those famous lines of Jesus' about His body and His blood.

Twelve men who had been companions for almost three years were not going to eat in silence! When Jesus arrived, He found them in a bitter contention among themselves as to which of them should be thought of as the greatest in heaven. With tact and gentleness, Jesus reproved their contentious spirit and started washing their feet. Incredulous, Simon Peter said, "Are You going to wash my feet, Lord? Never at any time will You wash my feet!"

It was just a gut reaction to the thought of the Master washing the feet of the servants, but it wasn't as wrenching a statement as Jesus made. "I tell you the truth, one of you is going to betray me" (John 13:21).

As His words reverberated around the table, rumblings among the apostles began as they speculated on who this despicable person could be. He would have to be the least among them, someone really low. Peter said to John, "Ask him which one he means" (v. 24).

When John asked, Jesus said, "I will dip some bread in the sauce and give it to him." He handed it to Judas, who left at once. Some of them thought Jesus was telling Judas to buy "what was needed for the Feast, or to give something to the poor" (v. 29), which shows they weren't listening. Instead, they were talking, so Jesus had to say Simon's name twice to get his attention. He had something important to say to Simon Peter.

a test is coming

Satan had demanded—and apparently received—permission to test the disciples just as he had requested permission from God to test the faith of Job. Jesus said, "Simon, Simon, behold, Satan has demanded permission to sift you like wheat" (Luke 22:31 NASB). In other words, the upcoming events when Jesus would be tried and crucified would shake up the disciples. The whole group faced testing that could not be avoided.

Jesus used the picture of the farmer separating the grain from the chaff to describe what Satan's sifting would be like. On the threshing floor, "the head and stalk of wheat were beaten and trampled. Then that finer broken mass was placed in small quantities in a sieve. By the violent shaking of the sieve, the straw was tested for any wheat content in it. As the wind blew the chaff away, the valuable wheat emerged from the violent shaking."[1]

The hours ahead were going to be trying ones for all the disciples, but Peter particularly would be shaken by the events. To him, Jesus softened His warning with assurance. Jesus said, "But I have prayed for you, Simon, that your faith may not fail" (Luke 22:32).

Why was Peter singled out for prayer? Wasn't Jesus concerned for all the disciples?

WHY PETER?

Jesus was very much concerned about all the disciples; the *you* in "to sift you as wheat" (v. 31) is plural. Later that evening, as we will see in the next chapter, Jesus prayed for all of them, but at this time, He mentioned having prayed for Peter. The reason Peter is singled out is his leadership role.

- In every listing of the twelve apostles in the New Testament, Peter is named first.
- Peter was in the inner circle of disciples, with James and John, and always was named first.
- On almost every occasion in which a spokesman for the group was needed, Peter was that spokesman.
- Peter was the first apostle to acknowledge that Jesus was the Messiah (Luke 9:20).
- To Peter Jesus said, "I will give you the keys of the kingdom" (Matthew 16:19).

"Preferred position always makes one most vulnerable to attack. Satan is always alert to the most effective way of accomplishing his purpose. To get a great one like Simon into his grasp and to use him as he was using Judas would be real victory."[2] Something, though, was going to keep that from happening, and the clue is in two little words.

173

"BUT I . . ."

Peter was going to be tested, but he was going to pass the test because Jesus prayed. After warning him, Jesus said, "*But I* have prayed for you, Simon, that your faith may not fail. And when you have turned back, strengthen your brothers" (Luke 22:32, italics added). Jesus dealt with Peter frankly and prophetically so that the other disciples might benefit. Satan would pass Peter through a sieve of temptations: but because of the intercession of Jesus, the chaff would be separated from the wheat and he would emerge as a strong leader, which he did.

- Peter assumed leadership of the disciples after Jesus' ascension.

- He made the first move to choose someone to replace Judas.

- He was the spokesman on the Day of Pentecost. He preached the first Christian sermon, and three thousand people became believers.

- He braved the rage of the Sanhedrin in his preaching and his healing.

- He went to Samaria when the gospel was first preached there.

- He received the Gentile Cornelius into the fellowship of the church and consequently was instrumental in opening the door for Gentiles to become believers.

- According to church tradition, he followed Jesus to prison and to a martyr's death on a cross.

Jesus' successful intercession on Peter's behalf is an encouraging reminder of what is possible when we pray for others. This isn't something that only Jesus could do. The possibility is there for all of us.

the POWER of INTERCESSION

When prayer is intense and vivid faith exists, your prayers may bring peace to an anxious heart or help others deal with difficulties or experience spiritual renewal. You don't have to be anybody special or have stellar qualifications, as these examples of ordinary people praying reveal.

A mother prayed. Before entering seminary, I worked for a summer as a recreation worker for a YMCA located in a low-income, high-crime-rate area of Chicago. During the last part of the summer when the resident director left for the YMCA resident camp, I was to fill her position. From what I had observed of the directorship, only a superhuman person could do that job, and I knew that I was no Wonder Woman.

On the day I was to make the transition from age-group worker to director, I awoke with a hard lump in my stomach. As I moved around the apartment, the lump turned to butterflies, and my stomach was in a whirl. I tried to eat breakfast but couldn't. I wanted to pray, but I was afraid no reassurance would come. Fear took over, and I broke into tears. After crying for a while, I finished dressing and went to work.

I had been at work about an hour when calmness came over me. Suddenly, the job did not look so formidable. I realized that I wasn't a superhuman, but I could do the job and perhaps do it quite well. There seemed to be no explanation for what happened. All I know is that I experienced relief. This had not come through my prayers because I had not prayed.

Two days later I received a letter from my mother. She had written it the morning I made the transition. She wrote, "Are you all right this morning? I have a feeling that something is wrong—that you need help, so I am praying for you."

Two students prayed. In her book, *Prayer Without Pretending*, medical missionary Anne J. Townsend wrote about how her marriage had become tense and strained.[3] Due to the pressure of their work as doctors, she and her husband had begun to drift apart. They rarely saw one another to communicate, as both were working full time and their off-duty hours rarely coincided. Their relationship was in danger of disintegrating because of neglect. While she was away for a month, her husband realized what was happening and met her at the airport. He was ready to talk.

On that same day, two medical students who frequently prayed for the Townsends felt compelled to stop what they were doing and pour out their hearts in prayer for them. The students didn't know why they were praying, and they didn't know for what, never suspecting that missionaries might have marital difficulties.

Their prayers, though, were the undergirding that the Townsends needed. They had only two days together before they were due back at the hospital on full-time duty. Much sorting out needed to be done, and practical steps had to be taken to ensure that they had time for each other in the future. After months of failure to communicate closely, it could have been hard for them suddenly to be frank and open with one another again if two medical students hadn't been praying. As it was, they were able to get their marriage back on track because two students prayed.

An invalid woman prayed. After the Chicago fire, evangelist Dwight L. Moody went to England to rest and to learn from the Bible scholars there. He had no plans to preach, but one Sunday morning he was persuaded to preach in a church in London. Everything about the service dragged. He wished that he had never consented to preach.

There was an invalid woman in the city who had heard of Mr. Moody's work in America and had been asking God to send him to London. This woman's sister was present at the church when Moody preached. When she got home, she asked her invalid sister to guess who had spoken for them that morning. She guessed one after another of those her pastor usually asked. Her sister said, "No, Mr. Moody from Chicago."

The sick woman turned pale, and said, "This is an answer to my prayer. If I had known that he was to be at our church, I should have eaten nothing this morning, but waited on God in prayer. Leave me alone this afternoon; do not let anyone come to see me; do not send me anything to eat."

All that afternoon that woman prayed. As Mr. Moody preached that night, he soon became conscious that there was a different atmosphere in the church. As the service drew to a close, Moody felt impressed to give an invitation. He asked all who would accept Christ to rise. Four or five hundred people stood up. He thought that they misunderstood him, and so he put the question several ways so there would be no mistake. But no, they had understood. He then asked them to go to an adjoining room. As they exited, he asked the pastor of the church who these people were. He replied, "I do not know."

In the adjoining room, Moody put the question very strongly, but still there were just as many who rose. The next day he left for Dublin, but no sooner had he arrived than he received a telegram from the pastor saying that he must return and help him, for a great revival had begun.[4]

Truly the prayers of righteous people are powerful and effective (James 5:16), but this doesn't mean that intercessory prayer is simple or without its mysteries. In fact, unless you take the long view—looking at Peter's role in the early church—it looks like Peters' faith failed.

the short view vs. the Long view

After Jesus' words of warning and reassurance, Peter proclaimed absolute loyalty to Jesus (Matthew 26:33,35). Peter said he was "ready to go to prison" and "to die" with Jesus (Luke 22:33). No greater statement of commitment could have been made. Peter may have expected Jesus to commend him for his loyalty. Instead, Peter heard a sober prediction. "Jesus answered, 'I tell you, Peter, before the rooster crows today, you will deny three times that you know me'" (v. 34). Peter did exactly as Jesus predicted.[5]

Because Peter denied Jesus, does that mean Peter's faith failed? And if it did, wouldn't that mean Jesus' prayer for Peter wasn't answered?

Some insist that it is a "no" answer to prayer. They have no problem looking at Jesus' prayer as one that was prayed sincerely and confidently but nevertheless was not answered "yes." Obviously, Peter was disloyal after Jesus prayed. No question about it—it was a "no" answer to prayer.

But looking at it as a "no" answer is hard for others. Surely, if anyone were to receive what he asked for in prayer, wouldn't it be Jesus? Consequently, others try to make a "yes" answer out of Peter's experience. For example, one Bible expositor said that Peter's faith did not fail; his hope did. He said Peter's faith did not fail when he was denying Jesus; neither did his love fail. What failed was his hope and, therefore, his courage. Peter's hope was dead. When hope is gone, courage fails, and cowardice sets in.

Although it is true that courage fails in the absence of hope, I believe this explanation is looking at Peter's situation unrealistically. It is as if the expositor were trying to read a solid "yes" into the situation, as if he could not possibly accept the fact that Jesus might have received a "no" answer.

There is a more realistic way of looking at the situation than either a "yes" or a "no" answer. Failure there would be, but not utter failure. Jesus seemed to know exactly what would happen. Satan might have been granted power to sift the disciples, but Jesus was confident that Satan would gain only *temporary victory*. Why was Jesus so certain of this? *Because He had prayed.* Jesus would not be discouraged by a momentary lapse of Peter's faith or despondent because of his denials. Jesus' prayer would hold Peter.

Notice the confidence Jesus expressed. He said, "*When* you turn back," not "*If* you turn back." "Turn back" means to reaffirm loyalty or retrace your steps. Jesus knew Peter was no calculating deserter. Peter was a man of limited foresight and uncertain responses who wasn't planning denial. His loyalty to Jesus would lapse temporarily, but it would return. Jesus was so sure of this that He had a purpose in mind for Peter. He said, "When you have turned back, strengthen your brothers" (Luke 22:33).

The other disciples, too, would be denying Jesus, only in a not so obvious way. Those who shared in the sifting ordeal

178

would feel their own failures deeply. They would need someone to help them reestablish their faith and their sense of direction and purpose. Peter, their leader, would know how they felt and would be able to help them. It was as if Jesus were saying to Peter, "You will deny Me, yes, but the result will be that you will be able to help your brothers who are going through the sifting, too."

The long view shows us Jesus' prayer was answered, and it is an answer that should help us with our praying.

not all answers are equal

The way God answered Jesus' prayer for Peter should help us understand some of the answers we receive to our prayers. When we pray for some "thing," it is easy to gauge when the answer comes. The answers are not so easy to discern when we are praying about intangibles, such as emotional or spiritual issues. The answer may not come in completed form but may well come in the form of a process, as it did with Peter. When praying for Peter's faith not to fail, Jesus was not asking that Peter be able to meet all of life with a blazing faith, never faltering and never doubting. The answer came as a process. When the process was completed, Peter's faith was stronger and healthier.

We must face honestly the paradox that, although we expect all prayers to be answered simply and directly, they are not always. We see this here and in the remaining chapters. Seeing that the answers to Jesus' prayers were not always what we would expect them to be should help keep us from being disillusioned and discouraged when similar answers come our way. The answer may be in the form of a process, as it was with Peter. Something more beautiful and stronger than we had hoped for might be produced in the lives of those we pray for, so hold on and keep praying. God is calling your name and calling it twice because He wants your attention. His message to you is, "John, John (or Jane, Jane), there is power in intercession. Your prayers can make a difference."

making the
CONNECTION

Who do I know who is experiencing Satan's violent sifting and could use the power of my intercession?

How can the fact that not all prayers are answered simply and directly help me when I pray for others?

Notes

1. Ray Summers, *Commentary on Luke* (Waco, Tex.: Word, 1972), 280.

2. Ibid., 279.

3. Anne J. Townsend, *Prayer Without Pretending* (Chicago: Moody, 1973), 74–75.

4. James G. K. McClure, *Intercessory Prayer: A Mighty Means of Usefulness* (Old Tappan, N.J.: Revell, 1902), 22–24.

5. Although they vary in order, all the Gospels give the sad account of the denials of Peter. See Matthew 26:58, 69–75; Mark 14:54, 66–72; Luke 22:54–62; John 18:15–27.

INTERCEDING
WITH LOVE

"Holy Father, protect them by the power of your name—the name you gave me—so that they may be one as we are one. . . .

I am coming to you now, but I say these things while I am still in the world, so that they may have the full measure of my joy within them. . . . the world has hated them. . . . My prayer is not that you take them out of the world but that you protect them from the evil one. . . . Sanctify them by the truth."

—John 17:11, 13–15, 17

When my children were preschoolers, I asked Rosie, the mother of a son who had just gotten married, "What was it like?"

She said, "It ranks right up there with the first day of school. On his wedding day I felt the same way I did when he boarded the school bus and the driver closed the door behind him. Oh, I would still be an influence in his life, but I wondered, *Have I done enough? Will he be all right? Will he succeed?*"

Three grown sons later, I now know what she meant. There's something about the first day of school, the first day of college when you leave your son at the dorm, the boarding of the bus headed for boot camp, and hearing him say "I do" that makes you very conscious of what you have and have not done as a parent. Right up to the time the bus or dorm door closes, you may still be trying to get in some last minute parenting, from "If you should have an emergency, you know what to do, don't you?" to "When you do your laundry, don't mix the colored clothes with the whites." All the while, your heart is filled with love for him and concern for his future. Will he be all right? Will he succeed?

I thought of this when I studied Jesus' prayer for all of His disciples—the one He prayed the night before His death. It had the flavor of a concerned parent. Only in this case, Jesus was the one going away. He was leaving His disciples behind and giving them enormous responsibility. Had He prepared them enough? Would they succeed?

THE NEED FOR PRAYER

During Passover Jesus gathered with the twelve apostles in a borrowed room of a friend's home to eat the Feast of Unleavened Bread. Acutely aware that the end was near, Jesus encouraged them to remember Him when He was gone with symbols of bread and wine. With a cup of wine in His hand, Jesus said, "This is my blood of the covenant, which is poured out for many. . . . I will not drink again of the fruit of the vine until that day when I drink it anew in the kingdom of God" (Mark 14:24–25).

The apostles did not have the same awareness of what was happening. They didn't understand all that was being said, and they couldn't figure out everything that was happening. Jesus said things they didn't understand. Judas left the group, and they weren't sure why. The eleven who remained were nervous and uneasy.

Not only was Jesus aware that His death was near, He was also conscious of the responsibility He was leaving with them. It would be up to them to see that His story survived, that men and women and boys and girls would know about Him and how they could find forgiveness of sin and eternal life. As eyewitnesses, they would provide the authentic record of Jesus' words and deeds. If they should fail, there was no other way of assuring the continuance of His story. Jesus had worked hard during their time together, but there were always interruptions. There was more they needed to know.

Aware of how the Eleven were feeling and yet conscious of what else they needed to know before He departed, Jesus comforted and taught them (John 14–16). He said He was going to prepare a place for them, and He promised to take them to that place (14:2–3). He said they would be able to perform greater works than He did (14:12). He tenderly called them orphans (14:18) and promised that someone, a Counselor (14:16, 26), would come so that they would still feel close to Him. He warned them of hard times, too. They would be persecuted because they associated with Him (15:18–16:4).

But as every parent knows, there comes a time when the words finally must end. There's no more time. The door to the bus closes, you say good-bye and get into the car for the drive home, and the minister says, "I now pronounce you man and wife." That's when you have to admit, "I have done all I can do. I have said all I can say. I commit you, my child, and your future to God." Jesus did this with a prayer (John 17) following His talk. Sprinkled throughout the prayer were references to what He had accomplished. It was as if He, too, were saying, "Here's what I have done, Father. It is all I could do in the time You gave me. I have said all I can say. Now I want to give to You those you gave to Me. I commit them to Your care and protection."

the prayer of commitment

Jesus began by praying for Himself (John 17:1–5)—a good place for any intercessor to begin. Most of us, when it is time to pray for others, are not living unencumbered lives. We usually have pressing concerns that command our attention, so it is best to go ahead and pray for those needs. When we give them to God, our energy is freed up so we can focus on the needs of others.

What was at the forefront of Jesus' mind was His desire that God glorify Him so He could glorify God (v. 1). And as in the case of Lazarus, it was in Jesus' death that the Son would be glorified and would therefore glorify the Father.

After reaffirming His desire to glorify God, Jesus prayed for the disciples, referring to them as "those whom you gave me" (vv. 6, 9). Jesus had revealed the character of God to these men, and the disciples had responded by recognizing that Jesus came from God and by obeying His words. Consequently, they were now the property and the concern of both the Father and the Son.

Full of gratitude and heartfelt concern for these men, Jesus said, "I pray for them" (v. 9). For what did He ask?

the petitions

When you think of the trauma, shock, and grief that the disciples were going to experience shortly, how would you have prayed for them? I suspect many of us would utter "God, be with" and "God, help" prayers as in "God, help them bear the shock. Comfort their hearts, and help them to go on." But these are not the kinds of things Jesus asked for. While He was concerned for their immediate needs, His greater concern was that His work—the mission God gave Him to do—be continued and expanded. For that the disciples would need unity, joy, protection, and dedication.

"Holy Father, keep them in Your name, the name which You have given Me, that they may be one even as We are" (John 17:11 NASB). Name, when referring to God, indicates His character or nature. Jesus had kept the disciples together working as a group by revealing God to them. Now He asked God to do this after He was gone. Only in this way could they work as a group and not be fragmented, which was a strong possibility. Judas had already split. James and John, the "Sons of Thunder" (Mark 3:17), may have had inherited tendencies toward angry outbursts. Peter was impetuous, not exactly a good trait for working with a group. One disciple belonged to the party

of the Zealots, meaning he had radical political leanings. On more than one occasion, the disciples quarreled about positions in Jesus' kingdom; in fact, they had done so during the feast that evening. When confusion and grief were added to this volatile mix, would the group disintegrate? If that should happen, God's work would be severely handicapped, perhaps stymied altogether, so Jesus prayed for them to be united.

"I say these things while I am still in the world, so that they may have the full measure of my joy within them" (John 17:13). To promote God's standards is to incur the hostility of the world. Jesus had told the disciples that they were different from the world. Their values were different from the world's values; their standards were different from the world's standards. Consequently, they would be hated, so Jesus wanted them to have joy. Jesus prayed that the joy which had been His might be fully theirs (15:11; 16:24). It would compensate for the world's hatred.

"My prayer is not that you take them out of the world but that you protect them from the evil one" (17:15). Satan would try to get Jesus' followers off course just as he had done with Jesus. One solution would be to take them out of the world, but if that were the case, the mission He launched would fail. To carry His work forward, they must stay in the world and witness to the world; therefore, Jesus prayed that God might protect them from the evil one.

"Sanctify them by the truth; your word is truth" (v. 17). Jesus prayed that the disciples might be consecrated in God's Word just as He was being consecrated through His death on the cross. (The Greek verb *hagiazo* can be translated "consecrated" as well as "sanctified.") His dedication was not in place of theirs, but it went before theirs and called for theirs. He wanted them to serve without reservation.

Jesus was so sure God would answer His requests that He went ahead and prayed for all future believers (vv. 20–26)— people who would trust in Him because the disciples continued His mission. Jesus' prayer of commitment showed confidence in God and confidence in His followers.

CONFIDENCE IN GOD

In manner and word, Jesus showed His faith in God. His manner of praying was conversational—the way you would talk with someone you are on intimate terms with. He called God "Father," "Righteous Father," and "Holy Father," denoting an awareness of God and who He is. When awareness of the other person is not present in a conversation, it becomes a monologue and usually a boring one.

His words reveal their long, close relationship. Jesus said they were together before the world was made (John 17:5), and He was anticipating going to the Father (v. 13). He said that God had loved Him before the world was made (v. 24), and He wanted the disciples to know that love (v. 26). He asked that the followers be one just as He and God were one (vv. 11, 22).

Jesus prayed as a loving parent would for a child wrapped in his or her arms, as if what He said and how He said it were also important. After all, the disciples were listening. This was not a prayer Jesus prayed in solitude. How reassuring His words and how comforting His manner must have been to them. That would give them something to cling to during the difficult days ahead. I know, because I've been the recipient of this kind of prayer many times, and I know its lingering effect.

One such time occurred while I was writing this book. Do you remember my describing in chapter 9 how anxious I became over a retreat I was planning? When I started giving thanks in advance, my anxiety level lessened but did not fully disappear. Because God had given me the vision for the retreat, I wanted to work in faith, not in fear. I tried various psychological tools to defeat it, but nothing worked, so I told Mary Rose and Cookie, two women with whom I meet for prayer frequently, about my anxiety.

They listened carefully as I spilled out my fears, and then they prayed fervently and boldly. I had been thanking God for the fifty women He was going to give me—the fifty needed to cover the bill for the retreat center; they asked Him for more than fifty. They also prayed that the retreat would be a great spiritual experience—for me and for the women who attended. Here I was worried only about paying the bills and they were praying for a movement of God.

My anxiety left, which is what I wanted and needed, but there was an additional blessing in the weeks that followed. Whenever there was a long lull between registrations, I would be tempted to be anxious again. That's when I would recall the fervor of the women's prayers, their faith, and their specific requests. Their prayers were seared on my memory in a way that ministered to me for weeks afterward. This added benefit wouldn't have been mine if they hadn't prayed for me in my presence.

When we pray for others in their presence, our ministry of intercession widens. Not only will those for whom we are praying experience God's answer to our prayers, they will feel our love and concern and be comforted. They will hear our words of confidence and be strengthened. Their hope will rise as they hear us express faith in God.

The thoughts, feelings, and desires we express in prayer can minister to those for whom we pray just as they must have ministered to the eleven apostles when Jesus prayed for them (John 17:6–19). How else would the words have stuck in John's memory for so long? By the time he wrote down Jesus' prayer, many years had passed. The prayer was probably said around A.D. 30, and John's Gospel wasn't penned until about A.D. 90. The prayer was seared on John's memory. And why not? It was a wonderful expression of love for the disciples and confidence in God.

I found Jesus' confidence in God understandable, considering their oneness and like-mindedness. As John would later write, "This is the confidence we have in approaching God: that if we ask anything according to his will, he hears us. And if we know that he hears us—whatever we ask—we know that we have what we asked of him" (1 John 5:14–15). Jesus certainly knew what God's will was.

But confidence in His followers was what I found hard to understand. How could that be, considering who they were and what they were like?

CONFIDENCE IN HIS FOLLOWERS

In His prayer in John 17, Jesus described the disciples in what seemed to me as "glowing terms."

- "They have obeyed your word" (v. 6).
- "They know that everything you have given me comes from you" (v. 7).
- "I gave them the words you gave me and they accepted them" (v. 8).
- "They knew with certainty that I came from you" (v. 8).
- "They believed that you sent me" (v. 8).
- "Glory has come to me through them" (v. 10).
- "They are not of the world, even as I am not of it" (v. 16).

As I read the Gospels, I don't see the disciples quite that way. For example, I don't see them as certain. When Jesus questioned them about who He was, only Peter answered, and he didn't fully grasp what he was saying. The disciples often misinterpreted who Jesus was and didn't grasp what His mission was.

Jesus described the disciples as being "not of the world," even as He was not of the world (vv. 14, 16). Earlier in His talk, Jesus said, "The prince of this world . . . has no hold on me" (14:30), but the disciples clung to their material dreams of an earthly kingdom and of their own prominence in it. They were ambitious, carefully counting the sacrifices they had made and expecting rewards.

With His request that the disciples be one as He and the Father were one (17:11), Jesus was expressing confidence that this group could work as a unit. Unity is something hard for any group to achieve, and it seemed to me it would be particularly hard for this group of temperamental personalities, especially in light of the huge task Jesus was leaving them with. Very soon they would all flee and leave Jesus to face His enemies alone, yet Jesus believed they could and would work together as a unified group.

Maybe I shouldn't have, but I had to ask, *Was Jesus wearing rose-colored glasses?* As I thought about it, I knew He was not because that wouldn't have been in line with His character. Jesus was looking at them through eyes of love. Have you ever had the experience of watching a rambunctious child—certainly not your own child—that was too energetic and too active for your taste, and yet the parent never noticed? The parent takes the child, the one you clearly see as out of control, in his arms, loves and caresses him, as if he were the grandest person on earth. You're thinking, *Can't this parent see this child needs discipline?* But you are looking at the child at the moment, and you see only what grates on your nerves. You weren't with that parent when the child was born; you weren't around yesterday when the child was well behaved; you don't see the child's potential nor share the parent's dream for the child's future. You don't love the child. Eyes of love make a difference.

Jesus had been with these men for almost three years. He knew them well. He remembered their commitment to leave behind families, homes, and businesses to follow Him. Many followers had come and gone, but these remained faithful. Oh, how that must have pleased Him! They were loyal followers, dedicated followers, followers who were receiving His message even if they didn't fully understand it. Sure, there were temporary lapses, but with His eyes—and heart—of love, Jesus didn't count that against them. They were growing, and He saw their potential for being the persons who would make sure His story was told and retold.

I found this insight about Jesus' seeing the disciples with eyes of love very comforting. I could feel tension leaving my body as I realized, *Maybe I'm doing better at following Christ than I thought. Perhaps my failures don't outshine my faithfulness. Maybe He isn't as critical of me as I am. Maybe He sees me as growing. I'll have to admit I'm not where I used to be. Maybe He sees more potential in me than I see in myself. Perhaps He does indeed have a purpose for my life.*

If this realization is true—and I believe it is—then a prayer Jesus prayed when He was departing and His disciples were staying continues to minister. His manner, His words, His confidence, and most of all, His love, speak to me. Do they speak to you?

making the
CONNection

If Jesus had prayed only for the immediate needs of His disciples, how would His prayer have been different?

Do my prayers for others more often reflect their short-term or long-term needs?

perpetual
intercession

"I pray also for those who will believe in me . . . that all of them may be one, Father, just as you are in me and I am in you. May they also be in us so that the world may believe that you have sent me . . . and have loved them even as you have loved me."

—*John 17:20–21; 23*

At some time or other, have you been discouraged about living the Christian life? Were you ever close to giving up? Did you despair over the lack of results from your caring, witnessing, or teaching? One Christian living in an area where professing Christians number about .3 percent of the population said it took him eight long years before he had a solid chat about spiritual matters with his closest neighbors. It was eight years of back-fence conversations, borrowing and lending, dinner invitations, and nights out together before his opportunity came. Even then that was only a start, a door opening but not a conversion.

During those times of discouragement, when you think nothing is ever going to come from your earnest efforts, do you ever wonder, *Is anyone praying for me?*

When you find it hard to go on, do you throw up your hands and ask, *Is some one out there praying for me?*

I've got good news for you: Someone has and is. Jesus has prayed for you and continues to pray for you.

Long, Loving Look

Those eyes of love that saw eleven disciples (John 17:6–19) saw you too. After He prayed for the Eleven the night before His death, He went on to pray for future believers, which includes *you*.

As Jesus looked ahead into the future, He saw in one comprehensive glance all those the Father was going to give Him through the coming centuries. He saw those who would believe in Him because the Eleven were faithful (v. 20) to witness. Those future believers would face the same basic perils as the Eleven because the nature of the world would remain the same. They would need the same undergirding of divine power; therefore, Jesus prayed for them too (vv. 20–26). For what did He ask?

Jesus prayed that all of them might be one. Odd request, isn't it? Considering all that believers would need to be faithful, why didn't Jesus pray for them to have courage? Why didn't He pray for them to be tenacious and persistent? Why didn't He pray for them to be bold and articulate? Why unity?

the power of unity

Jesus prayed for believers to be united so the world would know that God *sent Him* and that God *loved them* (vv. 21, 23). Unity is crucial to letting men and women know that God loves them so much that He gave His only Son so that they might have eternal life (John 3:16).

How can unity help with getting these messages across? Everyone knows it is more natural for people to be divided than to be united. It is more human for people to fly apart than to come together. If people unite and work together effectively in the name of someone, observers will notice. They will ask, Who is the person who unites these people? What is their cause? What draws them together?

We see an example of this after Jesus' death and resurrection when the disciples performed miracles, preached, and taught in His name. Some members of the Sanhedrin "were greatly disturbed because the apostles were teaching the people and proclaiming in Jesus the resurrection of the dead" (Acts 4:2). The Sanhedrin arrested them and made Peter and John stand before them. They questioned Peter and John, *"By what power or what name did you do this?"* (v. 7, italics added).

When Jesus prayed, that's the question He wanted nonbelievers in every age to ask. This is not to say that one person's actions will not prompt this question, but the greater notice— the greater power—will be evident when a group of people work together. The world recognizes how difficult it is to get people to unite, so when unity is readily visible, they are curious.

This kind of unity is not easily achieved. Unity among Christians—unity that will attract nonbelievers—requires a horizontal and a vertical connection.

The horizontal connection. When Jesus prayed for future believers to be united, He prayed that they would be one, just as He and the Father were one (John 17:21). Their model for unity is that which exists between the Father and the Son— distinct persons of the Godhead, but one in love, purpose, and will. The Father and the Son were united, and yet both kept the essence of who they were. When Jesus prayed for the Eleven to be unified, His intent was not for Peter, James, John, Matthew, Bartholomew, and the others to all be alike and never disagree. Likewise, Jesus was not asking for future believers to be a tight organization of clones. For unity to be effective and vibrant doesn't mean that everyone has to be alike or agree. It does mean being united in love, purpose, and will just as the Father and the Son were.

The vertical connection. Besides the horizontal connection, believers also need a vertical connection to be unified. They need to be linked *with* the Father and Son as indicated by Jesus' request, "May *they also* be in us" (John 17:21, italics added). They need this link so that they will have the supernatural strength needed to partner with other believers. As He said in His last talk with the disciples, "Apart from me you can do nothing" (15:5).

From His perspective Jesus wanted this link to be continuous, to extend beyond this life. He prayed, "Father, I want those you have given me to be with me where I am, and to see my glory" (17:24). He wanted an ongoing dynamic relationship with them that would result in their seeing His glory, the glory He had previously enjoyed before the creation of the world (v. 24).

When Jesus brought His prayer to a close (vv. 25–26), He indicated He would continue in His obedience to God, specifically the cross. That way the love with which God loved Him might find its home in the hearts of believers and He would find a home there as well, solidifying the vertical connection.

Jesus prayed for believers in every age—including you—to be horizontally and vertically connected so that men and women will know that God sent Jesus and that God loves them. When Jesus left earth and ascended to the Father, He did not stop praying. The risen Christ is at the right hand of God, making intercession for believers (Romans 8:34; Hebrews 7:25; 1 John 2:1).

THE INTERCESSION GOES ON

Jesus' prayer of intercession in John 17 is often referred to as Jesus' High Priestly Prayer because He entreated God on behalf of others. That is what the priests of the Old Testament did. They represented the people before God. As Jesus faithfully intercedes for believers, He continues in the role of High Priest.

The best picture we have of Jesus as the High Priest is in the book of Hebrews. This book was written to Christians who were declining spiritually (5:12–14; 6:8–9; 10:35).

The author [of Hebrews] . . . urged them not to cast away their confidence (10:35). They had been subjected to persecution and reproach, and to help them bear this "reproach of Christ," the writer reminds them, not only that Christ Himself had suffered (12:2), but also that they now have a great High Priest, Jesus the Son of God, who helps them in time of need (4:14–16; 5:1–5; 12:2–4). [1]

Like the Hebrew Christians, we are always in danger of declining spiritually. We worship an invisible God and in our weariness may debate His realness. To seriously try to follow Christ is to experience ridicule and friction, so sometimes we question if it is worth it. We may feel overwhelmed by hazards in our path; the obstacles to doing God's will just seem too large to scale. We may be tempted to get off track or to give up working with other believers who are different from us or disagree with us. The fact that we don't is because Jesus is praying for us. "But for the intercession of Jesus there would not necessarily be perpetuity in our faith."[2]

As lovely as the thought of Jesus praying for us is, it is nevertheless a hard concept to grasp. How Jesus could intercede for every believer is mind-boggling. While we may never understand how Jesus intercedes for us, we can believe it and count on it. Some of us can do this more readily than others. For some it seems to be a remote concept. If it is, here are some ways you can increase your awareness of His praying for you.

- Memorize and recite such Bible verses as Romans 8:34 and Hebrews 7:25, which deal with Jesus' role as intercessor.

- Meditate on Jesus' intercessory role when you take communion. The night Jesus prayed for the disciples is when He instituted the Lord's Supper as a memorial meal.

- Acknowledge His intercessory role when you pray. You might say something like this: "Heavenly Father, I know that Jesus is there at Your right hand. I know You are listening to Him as He pleads my case. I trust You to answer and to respond to Him because He was obedient and because You want me to know that You sent Him and You love me."

- Speak directly to Jesus in your prayers about His role. "Lord Jesus, I know right now as I am praying that You are praying right along with me. I know You understand my plight because You know what it is like to walk this earth. You walked around in human skin; You've worked at a job, lived with a family, tried to motivate people, and had a lot of demands made on You. In my weariness, I'm trusting You to plead my case with the Father."

Increasing our awareness of Jesus' High Priestly role increases the benefit we gain from His intercession. We are comforted knowing He cares and is entreating God on our behalf; but not to worry, His intercession is not dependent on our awareness. His intercession goes on whether or not we're aware of it, because He loves us. His praying for us prevents us from unravelling altogether in our times of trial. So on those days when you are tempted to throw in the towel and don't, it is because Jesus is praying. On those days when you wonder, *Is anyone praying for me?* you can stop and say out loud, "Yes, Jesus is praying for me."

Jesus exercises this priestly function without interruption or interference. He is a "priest forever" (Hebrews 7:17), and He "continueth ever," having "an unchangeable priesthood" (v. 24 KJV). He is a perpetual intercessor; therefore, there is never a single moment when His prayers for you do not reach our heavenly Father. What a comfort! And what a challenge!

the challenge of his intercession

While I am comforted by the thought of Jesus' intercession for me, I am also challenged by it. If I take seriously the admonition to follow Jesus' example, I have to ask myself some tough questions.

To what extent are the concerns of Jesus' intercessions reflected in my prayers? When Jesus prayed for Peter, He prayed that his faith would not fail. When He prayed for the eleven disciples, He prayed they would be unified, full of His joy, sanctified, and protected from the Evil One. When He prayed for future believers, He prayed for us to be unified as He and the Father were and vitally linked to the Godhead.

I confess: Not much of this terminology has found its way into my prayers for others. My prayers for others are more crisis-centered: a test to pass, a meeting that might fail, a crucial job interview, troubling emotions, debilitating sickness, a cancer diagnosis, upcoming surgery, traveling mercies. It is not wrong to pray for these things; after all, the Bible encourages us to cast all our cares on Him (1 Peter 5:7); however, Jesus' example reminds me that I need to be praying about faith issues.

Perhaps instead of protection on the road, I should sometimes be asking for protection from the Evil One. Instead of physical health, perhaps I should be praying for spiritual health. Instead of release from stress, maybe I should be praying for joy amid the turmoil. Christ's petitions were for spiritual benefits, and His example bids me to expand how I pray for others.

How long am I willing to pray? One Sunday morning I was half-listening to Byron give a devotion in an assisted living center where our Sunday school class was holding services. My ears perked up when he started talking about how he faithfully prayed for his grown children every day. At the time I was in the throes of praying for one of my college-age sons who was getting off track spiritually. As I listened to Byron, whose children were older than mine, I suddenly saw the need for intercession going on and on and on.

There are some burdens that come along in a prayer's life which we need to pray about and then release to God. If we didn't, our faith would be affected, our joy in praying would cease, and we would find ourselves uttering vain repetitions. There are other times, though, when we need to pray and pray as we need to for our children. Besides children, we may need our prayers for others to be on a long-term, ongoing basis.

- Missionaries
- Persons in authority
- World leaders
- Christians who are being persecuted
- Christian workers
- Our parents and other family members
- Our friends

I don't have any illusions that I can ever be the long-term intercessor that Jesus is, but His example inspires me to stretch the length of time I pray for others.

Do I understand that my prayers for others may not be answered simply and directly? In his book *The Lord's Prayers,* Elton Trueblood said, "There is . . . a sense in which Christ's prayer for the unity of His Church has not been answered affirmatively during all the succeeding centuries of conflict and strain."[3]

At times in my past, I've agreed with Trueblood that Jesus' prayer has not been answered. My reason had to do with my definition of unity—Christians being alike and tightly organized as a group. When I looked around, I didn't see that happening. When I read Christian history, it was full of stories of conflict and differences. I assumed that Jesus was still waiting for us to get our act together, and when that day came, His prayer would be answered.

But as I've studied Jesus' prayer life for this book, I had to reconsider. Perhaps His prayer has and is being answered because there has always been a faithful remnant of believers, united in love, purpose, and will. Otherwise, how would we now know of God's purpose and love? Sometimes the remnant has been large and sometimes small, but always some believers have united in love, purpose, and will so that the world would know that Jesus came from God and that God loves them.

The unity of the early believers is an example of what looks like disunity but isn't. They were continually threatened with incidents that could have torn them apart.

- The deception of Ananias and Sapphira (Acts 5)
- The quarrel over the distribution of food to the poor (Acts 6)
- The intense quarrel over the status of Gentile Christians (Acts 15:1–35)
- Paul and Barnabas' disagreement over John Mark (Acts 15:36–41)
- The divisions in the church at Corinth (1 Corinthians 1.10 17; 3:1–4; 6:1–8)

But the believers persevered. In the name of Jesus, they separated from Judaism and developed into a distinctively Christian group. Although threatened with disagreements, early believers survived and endured as a united body—the church—because Jesus prayed for them.

I don't know whether Jesus' prayer is an answered one or not, but seeing both possibilities is a reminder to me that we may not always be able to gauge an answered prayer when interceding for others. This encourages me to pray on when I don't see any results. One of the reasons I am a stronger personal prayer than an intercessor is because I *know* when God answers *my* prayers, but I don't have that certainty when I pray for others. When I pray, I'm expecting certain results that spell ANSWERED PRAYER, but I may not see those results. That's when I'm tempted to quit, and that's when I need to remember Jesus' prayer wasn't answered simply and directly either, but God's will was and is being achieved.

In every generation, some believers are united, patterning their unity after the oneness of the Father and the Son and connecting themselves with the Godhead in such a way that the world knows God sent Jesus and that God loves them. I want to be a part of this generation of united believers, consequently I choose to align myself with them and pray for them. It's a challenge, but the comfort is, I do not pray alone.

making the
CONNECTION

What difference does the knowledge that Jesus is praying for me make in my ability to be a faithful Christian?

What is one way I may increase my awareness of Jesus' intercessory role?

Notes

1. James G. S. S. Thomson, *The Praying Christ* (Grand Rapids: Eerdmans, 1959), 106.
2. B. H. Carroll, *Messages on Prayer* (Nashville: Broadman, 1942), 52.
3. Elton Trueblood, *The Lord's Prayers* (New York: Harper & Row, 1965), 96.

maɢnanimous
intercession

*When they came to the place called the Skull, there they crucified him.
. . . Jesus said, "Father, forgive them, for they do not know what they are
doing."*

—Luke 23:33–34

In the instances of Jesus' intercession that we have
looked at, we first saw Him praying for Lazarus, a close
friend; and Peter, a beloved follower. Then we listened
in as He prayed for the disciples—both present and
future ones. Now, in this chapter, we see Him praying
for people who are cruel, insulting, uncaring, and mean.
We can understand His praying for Lazarus, Peter, and
the disciples—people whom He loved and who loved
Him in return. It is natural to pray for those we care
about—but pray for people who are cruel and unjust?
This isn't natural, especially when they are physically
hurting you, as they were Jesus. At the time, He was
being nailed to the cross.

from gethsemane to the cross

After Jesus prayed for His present and future disciples, He went to the Garden of Gethsemane to pray about His own needs. As He finished, a large crowd arrived. They were armed with swords and clubs and were intent on finding Him. Judas led the group. Earlier he had arranged a signal with them: "The man I kiss is the one you want."

After Judas kissed Jesus, the chief priests, the elders, and the temple police arrested Him. They whisked Jesus away for hastily arranged trials before the Sanhedrin. Ignoring their own judicial standards, the members didn't seek any witnesses on Jesus' behalf. They paid false witnesses to testify against Him and found Him guilty on false charges. Then they took Him to the Roman procurator, Pontius Pilate—a step necessary to legally bring about Jesus' death.

Pilate sensed that Jesus was innocent, but not wanting to court disfavor with the Jews, he tried to avoid making a decision. He sent Jesus to Herod Antipas, Pilate's Galilean counterpart, who was in Jerusalem for the Passover. Herod sent Jesus back to Pilate. Roman soldiers tormented Jesus during His appearances before both Pilate and Herod. They stripped Him of His clothes and forced Him to wear a crown of thorns.

Still convinced of Jesus' innocence but wanting to please the Jews, Pilate gave the crowd a choice. "Which one do you want me to set free? Barabbas or Jesus called the Christ?"

"Barabbas!" they shouted.

"Then what shall I do with Jesus?" Pilate asked.

They answered, "Crucify Him! Crucify Him!"

Pilate gave in and sentenced Jesus to death. Pilate had Jesus whipped and then turned Him over to the executioners. They immediately took Him to the crucifixion site.

It was then, as they drove the spikes through Jesus' hands and feet, that He prayed for His tormentors and enemies. He prayed for all those who contributed to His suffering and death. His heart of love took in all of them. What an unnatural response!

the natural response

What is your response when someone wrongs you, insults you, or hurts you? For most of us, our first impulse is to strike back and to get even. We want to defend ourselves. We are angry, and we want justice done. We may rant and rave over our frustration or we may simmer on the inside. We want to pay back those who hurt us, return evil for evil. We want to hurl accusations and make them realize the awfulness of what they have done.

Most crucifixion victims responded this way. They yelled, cursed, and even spat on their tormentors. But no evil word escaped the lips of Jesus. He responded to His tormentors and executioners by asking God to forgive them. That in itself is remarkable enough, but Jesus expressed these words while experiencing pain, hearing taunts, seeing callous faces, and feeling their ridicule. It is one thing to pray for an enemy across town, over the sea, or out of sight. But Jesus' enemies were in His face, and still He responded with, "Father, forgive them" (Luke 23:34).

To that request, He added a curious phrase: "For they do not know what they are doing" (v. 34). To me, it looks as if they knew exactly what they were doing. From the time Jesus started breaking the Sabbath rules, the religious leaders began plotting to get Him (Matthew 12:14). After He raised Lazarus from the dead, the Sanhedrin was intent on killing Him (John 11:47–53). Their arrangement with Judas, their hastily held trials, and their breaking their own rules spells D–E–L–I–B–E–R–A–T–E. The Jewish people made a choice when Pilate offered them Barabbas instead of Jesus. Their passionate cry, "Crucify Him! Crucify Him!" says they would settle for nothing less than Jesus' death. To me, this deliberateness would be the hardest part to deal with. It is much easier to forgive insult, injury, and hurt when it is not done intentionally.

Considering the number of people involved, how they treated Him, and their deliberateness, Jesus was generous in His response. He was magnanimous.

THE MAGNANIMOUS RESPONSE

Magnanimity means generous in forgiving. The generous part could refer either to the times of forgiving or the amount of injuries that must be forgiven. A magnanimous person is generous in overlooking injury or insult; he is free from petty resentfulness or vindictiveness. Magnanimity suggests greatness of mind or soul, especially as shown in generously overlooking injuries.

The Crucifixion was the greatest crime in human history. Whenever the early New Testament preachers spoke of it, a kind of shocked horror was in their voices. The Roman governor himself was well aware that the Crucifixion was rank injustice. Jesus did not respond to this injustice with vindictiveness; instead, He responded with a prayer asking forgiveness for those who wronged Him.

Such a loving heart and such a generous prayer—and yet some question if Jesus even said it. This is because the prayer is not in the early manuscripts of the New Testament; your Bible may have a footnote to that effect. Believing it to be an insertion added to the original text, some scholars do not regard the prayer as authentic.

Whether Jesus actually uttered the words "Father, forgive them," the prayer is consistent with His life and teachings. A magnanimous spirit was a part of His nature. He gently treated the adulteress who was about to be stoned (John 8:1–11). In His Sermon on the Mount, He said, "If someone strikes you on the right cheek, turn to him the other also" (Matthew 5:39); "Love your enemies and pray for those who persecute you" (5:44); and "Do not judge, or you too will be judged" (7:1). When teaching His followers about prayer, Jesus said, "If you forgive men when they sin against you, your heavenly Father will also forgive you. But if you do not forgive men their sins, your Father will not forgive your sins" (6:14–15). On one occasion, when Peter asked, "How many times shall I forgive my brother when he sins against me? Up to seven times?" Jesus answered, "I tell you, not seven times, but seventy-seven times" (18:21–22).

Jesus' life and teachings demonstrate His magnanimous spirit, and it is one that we are to imitate. He taught us, "Love your enemies, do good to those who hate you, bless those who curse you, pray for those who mistreat you" (Luke 6:27–28, emphasis added). The message is clear that a forgiving spirit should characterize Christians, so it is not a question of *should* we be magnanimous intercessors. It is a question of *how*.

HOW to PRAY

The reason we have to ask "how" is because magnanimous intercession is a challenge. When we pray for people we care about, appropriate feelings are present to spur us on: concern, love, compassion, and sympathy. When someone hurts us or wrongs us, we are angry, resentful, hurt, and frustrated, which does little to motivate us to pray. Besides, we figure, if we pray for them, it will be as if what they did does not matter, as if we have to tolerate anything that happens to us. If we pray for them, they may never know that we prayed, let alone acknowledge it or appreciate it. What can we learn from Jesus' prayer that will help us with this challenge?

Start with words. Jesus' example suggests a helpful tool. Jesus didn't pray, "Father, help Me to forgive those who have brought about My death."[1] Instead, He prayed, "Father, forgive them."

These are good words for us to use in getting started when we do not feel like praying for those who hurt us. We do not have to begin with "*I forgive*"; we can begin with "*Father,* forgive them." When we take the right actions, the right emotions will follow.

If Jesus' words do not feel like our words, then try to say something that reflects the essence of Jesus' prayer. Stephen, the first Christian martyr, said, "Lord, do not hold this sin against them" (Acts 7:60) when he was being stoned to death.

My neighbor Jay prayed for an enemy by voicing different possibilities. His work supervisor was egotistical, argumentative, overbearing, sneaky, and at times, dishonest. He made life miserable for all the workers by continually belittling them. Jay grieved for himself and for the other workers. Everyone hated the supervisor.

Jay was at his wit's end and about ready to resign his job when a guest speaker at his church challenged him to pray for his enemies. The next morning on his way to work Jay tried to pray, but words wouldn't come. Finally he said, "Father, if the problem is me, change me. If it is the supervisor, change him."

Every day it was difficult to get the words out, but Jay repeated them. It was a full two weeks before he could say them readily. Along the way his attitude softened. After several months he began to sense a change in himself and in the supervisor.

Leave the punishment to God. With some wrongs we experience, we are going to be able to hold people accountable for their actions. Jay not only prayed, but he spoke with his supervisor. He asked him to quit belittling his work. In some cases, though, we will not be able to do anything, and that is when we need to leave the punishment to God.

Jesus prayed for God's forgiveness for His tormentors and executioners because they were going to need it. Jesus knew that those who abused Him and ridiculed Him would be held accountable for their actions. Early New Testament preachers verify this. They tried to stab men's minds with the realization of the sheer crime of the cross. Every mention of the Crucifixion in Acts is instinctive with horror at the crime committed (compare Acts 2:23; 3:13–15; 4:10; 5:30).

Praying *"Father,* forgive them" acknowledges that what people do does matter. In a world where men and women hurl injustices on others, God will hold them accountable and execute punishment (Romans 12:19). Many Bible scholars believe that when the Romans destroyed Jerusalem and obliterated its inhabitants at about the year A.D. 70, God was punishing them for putting Jesus to death.

To quicken our belief that God will hold those who wronged us accountable, we may need to acknowledge this as a part of our prayer.

"Father, forgive Sam for wasting our investment money that we trusted him with. I am trusting You that in Your time You will hold him accountable. I leave his punishment to You."

"Lord, forgive the customer who lashed out at me about his bill. I am trusting You to help her know how much words can hurt, and I'm counting on Your Spirit to lead her to repentance."

Try to gain insight concerning those who wronged you. Take Jesus' words "for they do not know what they are doing" as a cue rather than a puzzle. Jesus saw those who caused Him to suffer as responding to the circumstances and forces around them. Pilate did not follow his conscience because of past skirmishes with the Jews. He didn't want to risk being reported to Caesar and possibly losing his position. The executioners were doing their jobs. They were unaware of the dreadful consequences of their acts. The Jews were devoted to the ceremonial restrictions of the Law. They were blinded by years of tradition concerning what they perceived God to be like, blinded by what was really a fabrication. They did not, in their ignorance, know that they were bringing suffering and death to the Son of God.

If we can gain insight concerning those who have wronged us, we gain a valuable tool for forgiving them. What forces shaped their lives? What drove them to do what they did? If we could know all that is in their hearts, if we could walk in their shoes for a while, perhaps seeing some of their pain, we might be more tender in our judgment.

I wonder if this isn't one reason Jesus suggested confrontation when forgiveness is needed (Matthew 18:15; Luke 17:3). Confrontation leads to communication. In talking with the person who wronged us, we may gain understanding of the forces that shaped and motivated him or her. Pray before meeting with the person.

Magnanimity does not suggest that wrongdoers go scot-free, but it does call for understanding the pressures that led to the wrongdoing. When we do, this will help us pray as Jesus did: "Father, forgive them, for they do not know what they are doing."

Don't expect simple answers. Usually when we intercede for someone, we pray with the expectation that it will make a difference in the person's life. That is as it should be; there is power in intercession as we saw in the chapter 15.

When we pray for our enemies, our prayer might make a big difference in someone's life, some difference, or no difference at all. When Jay prayed for his supervisor, the supervisor changed some, but it was not a dramatic or complete change. The work situation improved, but it was still not perfect. The supervisor had deep-rooted personality problems and was involved in deviant social behavior that continued to make him prone to antagonistic behavior.

Some Bible scholars say that Jesus' prayer for God to forgive those who caused Him to suffer and to die was not answered because Jerusalem was later punished. Others say it was partially answered. Many who were present and involved in Jesus' crucifixion accepted God's forgiveness in those early days of Christianity, but many did not. They continued to stubbornly resist recognizing Jesus as the Son of God.

I believe Jesus' prayer was answered; it just wasn't answered *simply*. Through Jesus' death, forgiveness became available to everyone—to those who contributed to Jesus' suffering and to the rest of us. That does not mean that men and women automatically enter into a right relationship with God, but it means that forgiveness is available. It is up to men and women to receive God's forgiveness.

I mention this not to dilute your enthusiasm for prayer but to recognize that the greatest benefit that may occur from your magnanimous intercession for others is not what happens to them, but what happens to *you*.

WHAT'S IN IT FOR YOU

What happens when we pray as Jesus prayed? How will praying for those who hurt us help us?

Our feelings change. Several months of praying changed

Jay's feelings. Instead of counting the wrongs the man did, he looked at him with mercy, genuinely feeling sorry for him. Jay was no longer filled with anger and grief. When we pray for those we hate, we begin to hate them less. When we pray for those we resent, we mellow in our attitude.

We keep our channel of receptivity clear. To not pray for those who wrong us is to provide fertile ground for growing resentment and bitterness. These swell and fill up our inner space, hampering God's ability to bless us. We see this principle in Jesus' teaching, "If you forgive men when they sin against you, your heavenly Father will also forgive you. But if you do not forgive men their sins, your Father will not forgive your sins" (Matthew 6:14–15). God's forgiveness is available, but unforgiveness blocks our being able to experience it.

We grab hold of the breadth of the love of God. When the wrongs against us are great and we pray as Jesus' did, we are able to identify with the heart of Jesus. As we think about what He experienced and how much He was tormented and how terribly He was treated, our hearts will be touched by the depth of His love for them and for us. I know I was as I studied this prayer. I was so touched by Jesus' love that I couldn't find words to describe it. As an old gospel song states, "His love is greater than tongue or pen can ever tell."

We take on some of the divine nature. I asked a person who I knew had been hurt and wronged by people in the past, "Barry, have you ever prayed for your enemies?"

Barry answered, "Absolutely not!"

Momentarily caught off guard by such a strong answer, I was speechless.

Barry went on. "When you pray for your enemies is when you truly cross to the divine state, and I am not there."

No, I thought to myself, *but you could be moving toward it.* Jesus said that when we pray for our enemies, we become sons of the heavenly Father (Matthew 5:45). A "son of God" means a godlike person. When we are benevolent and magnanimous, we take on His nature and grow to be like Him. Alexander Pope's maxim is true: "To err is human, to forgive divine."

So if you want to change your feelings, keep your receptivity channel clear, grab hold of God's love, and grow in your likeness of Him; then hear again Jesus praying for forgiveness for those who crucified Him, and follow His example. When an unforgiving spirit threatens to turn your heart to bitterness, then pray, "Father, forgive them, for they do not know what they are doing."

making the
CONNECTION

How can Jesus' example help me to forgive when it seems impossible?

What can I pray when I can't say, "I forgive"?

Note

1. This is not to suggest that Jesus wasn't expressing His forgiveness when He prayed. This would be inconsistent with who He was and what He taught.

epilogue

We started this study together because we wanted to learn from Jesus. We wanted to reach heaven as He did and have God respond with power and direction. Our request was, "Lord, teach us to pray."

Now that we have completed the study, we know four key components to reaching heaven:

- *Withdrawal.* Jesus repeatedly withdrew for prayer —most of the time alone but sometimes with His disciples. Jesus needed those times to clarify God's purpose in every situation and to receive the power He needed to accomplish God's will.

- *Thanksgiving.* Jesus laced His living with thanksgiving. In good times, bad times, and challenging times, Jesus had a heart of gratitude that reflected His trust and confidence in God.

- *Honesty.* Jesus spoke honestly to God about the most personal dimensions of His life. "He offered up prayers and petitions with loud cries and tears to the one who could save him from death, and he was heard because of his reverent submission" (Hebrews 5:7).

- *Intercession.* Jesus was concerned not only about reaching heaven for Himself but also about reaching it for others, so He prayed for His followers. He prayed with love, consistency, and magnanimity so they could receive God's power and direction.

These cornerstones were indispensable to Jesus' prayer life, and the challenge before us is to make them indispensable to ours.

One commentator underscored the preposition *to* in the request, "Lord, teach us to pray." He said that when the disciples asked Jesus to teach them *to* pray, they were actually asking Jesus to *make* them pray. "We have seen what it does in your life, Lord. Now make us pray like You and we'll receive what you receive." In light of our nature, it's understandable that the commentator would make such a remark. All the knowledge in the world will not help us in our prayer life unless we are willing to incorporate what we've learned. This is truly a case where learning will be achieved by doing, so let's imitate Jesus. Let's "approach the throne of grace with confidence, so that we may receive mercy and find grace to help us in our time of need" (Hebrews 4:16).

appendix

jesus' prayers in order of their occurrence

Order Based On
*A Harmony of the Gospels for Students of the
Life of Christ*
by A. T. Robertson

Prayed at His baptism (Matthew 3:13–17; Mark 1:9–11; Luke 3:21–23).

Withdrew to pray when the crowds in Capernaum wanted Jesus to stay with them (Mark 1:35–39; Luke 4:42–43).

Withdrew to pray after healing the leper (Matthew 8:2–4; Mark 1:40–45; Luke 5:12–16).

Prayed before choosing the Twelve (Mark 3:13–19; Luke 6:12–16).

A prayer of thanks after working with people who rejected His miracles (Matthew 11:25–26).

Gave thanks before the feeding of the 5,000 (Matthew 14:15–21; Mark 6:36–44; Luke 9:12–17; John 6:5–13).

Withdrew for prayer following the feeding of the 5,000 (Matthew 14:22–23; Mark 6:45–46; John 6:14–15).

Gave thanks before the feeding of the 4,000 (Matthew 15:32–38; Mark 8:1–9).

Prayed before questioning the apostles about His identity (Matthew 16:13–20; Mark 8:27–30; Luke 9:18–21).

Prayed before His transfiguration (Matthew 17:1–8; Mark 9:2–8; Luke 9:28–36).

A prayer of joy and thanksgiving after the return of the 70 (KJV, NASB) or 72 (NIV) (Luke 10:17–21).

Prayed before His disciples asked to be taught to pray (Luke 11:1).

Gave thanks at Lazarus' grave (John 11:36–44).

Blessed the little children (Matthew 19:13–15; Mark 10:13–16; Luke 18:15–17).

Prayed when His heart was troubled (John 12:20–36).

Prayed for Peter (Luke 22:31–34).

Prayed at the institution of the Lord's Supper (Matthew 26:26–29; Mark 14:22–25; Luke 22:19–20; 1 Corinthians 11:23–26).

Prayed for the Holy Spirit (John 14:16–18).

Jesus' High Priestly Prayer (John 17) for His disciples.

Prayer for escape in the Garden of Gethsemane (Matthew 26:36–46; Mark 14:32–42; Luke 22:39–46).

Prayers from the cross:

- "Father, forgive them, for they do not know what they are doing" (Luke 23:33–34).

- "My God, my God, why have you forsaken me?" (Matthew 27:45–46; Mark 15:33–34).

- "Father, into your hands, I commit my spirit" (Luke 23:46).

- "It is finished" (John 19:30).

Blessed the bread with the disciples from Emmaus (Luke 24:30–32).

Parting blessing (Luke 24:50–51).

BIBLIOGRAPHY

Barclay, William. *The Gospel of John.* 3rd ed., 2 vols. The Daily Study Bible. Edinburgh: Saint Andrew, 1964.

———. *The Gospel of Luke.* 3rd ed. The Daily Study Bible. Edinburgh: Saint Andrew, 1964.

———. *The Gospel of Mark.* 2d ed. The Daily Study Bible. Edinburgh: Saint Andrew, 1956, 1964.

———. *The Gospel of Matthew.* 2d ed. 2 vols. The Daily Study Bible. Edinburgh: Saint Andrew, 1958, 1965.

———. *The Mind of Jesus.* New York: Harper & Row, 1960, 1961.

Carroll, B. H. *Messages on Prayer.* Compiled by J. W. Crowder and edited by J. B. Cranfill. Nashville: Broadman, 1942.

Claypool, John R. *The Light Within You.* Waco, Tex.: Word, 1983.

———. "Anxiety, Gratitude and Trust." A Sermon preached at Northminster Baptist Church, Jackson, Miss., 23 November 1980.

———. "Bearing One Another's Burdens." A Sermon preached at Northminster Baptist Church, Jackson Miss., 10 June 1979.

————. "The Power of Gratitude," A Sermon preached at Broadway Baptist Church, Fort Worth, Tex., 23 November 1975.

Coleman, Robert E. *The Mind of the Master.* Old Tappan, N.J.: Revell, 1977.

Corbishley, Thomas. *The Prayer of Jesus.* Garden City, N.Y.: Doubleday, 1977.

Denny, Randal Earl. *In the Shadow of the Cross.* Kansas City, Mo.: Beacon Hill, 1995.

Hallesby, Ole. Translated by Clarence J. Carlsen. *Prayer.* Minneapolis: Augsburg, 1994.

Hendricks, William L. *Who Is Jesus Christ?* Layman's Library of Christian Doctrine, vol. 2. Nashville: Broadman, 1985.

Hester, Hurbert Inman. *The Heart of the New Testament.* Nashville: Broadman, 1950, 1963.

Jeremias, Joachim. *The Prayers of Jesus.* Philadelphia, Pa.: Fortress, 1967.

Keener, Craig S. *The IVP Bible Background Commentary New Testament.* Downers Grove, Ill.: InterVarsity, 1993.

Keller, W. Phillip. "Solitude for Serenity and Strength," *Decision,* August–December 1981, 8–9.

Lockyer, Herbert. *All the Prayers of the Bible.* Grand Rapids: Zondervan, 1959.

McClure, James G. K. *Intercessory Prayer: A Mighty Means of Usefulness.* Old Tappan, N.J.: Revell, 1902.

Magdalen, Margaret. *Jesus, Man of Prayer.* Downers Grove, Ill.: InterVarsity, 1987.

Mitchell, Curtis C. *Praying Jesus' Way.* Old Tappan, N.J.: Revell, 1977.

Morris, Leon. *The Gospel According to St. Luke*. Tyndale New Testament Commentaries, vol. 3. Grand Rapids: Eerdmans, 1974.

Myra, Harold. *Surprised by Children*. Grand Rapids: Zondervan, 2001.

Osborne, Millard. "The Word of Loneliness," *The Way of the Cross and Resurrection*. Edited by John M. Drescher. Scottdale, Pa.: Herald, 1978.

Poinsett, Brenda. *Not My Will but Thine*. Nashville: Broadman & Holman, 1998.

———. *When Jesus Prayed*. Nashville: Broadman, 1981.

———. *Prayerfully Yours*. Nashville: Broadman, 1979.

Redding, David A. *Before You Call I Will Answer*. Old Tappan, N.J.: Revell, 1985.

Robertson, A. T. *A Harmony of the Gospels for Students of the Life of Christ*. New York: Harper, 1922, 1950.

Rodgers, Joni. "Bald in the Land of Big Hair," *Good Housekeeping*, March 2001, 165–67, 170–73.

Shepard, J. W. *The Christ of the Gospels: An Exegetical Study*. Grand Rapids, Mich.: Eerdmans, 1956.

Spencer, William David, and Aída Besançon Spencer. *The Prayer Life of Jesus: Shout of Agony, Revelation of Love, A Commentary*. Lanham, Md.: Univ. Press of America, 1990.

Stein, Robert H. *Jesus the Messiah: A Survey of the Life of Christ*. Downers Grove, Ill.: InterVarsity, 1996.

Summers, Ray. *Commentary on Luke*. Waco, Tex.: Word, 1972.

R. V. G. Tasker, *The Gospel According to St. Matthew*. Tyndale New Testament Commentaries, vol. 1. Grand Rapids: Eerdmans, 1961.

Terrell, Lloyd Preston. "The Emotional Prayers of Jesus," *Pray!* September-October 1999.

The Broadman Bible Commentary. General Articles, Matthew–Mark. Vol. 8. Nashville: Broadman, 1969.

The Broadman Bible Commentary. Luke–John. Vol. 9. Nashville: Broadman, 1969.

The Interpreter's Bible. Vol. 7. Nashville: Abingdon, 1955.

The Interpreter's Bible. Vol. 8. Nashville: Abingdon, 1955.

Thomas, Gary. "Giving Thanks." *Moody,* November–December 1996, pages 58–61.

Thomson, James G. S. S. *The Praying Christ.* Grand Rapids: Eerdmans, 1959.

Townsend, Anne J. *Prayer Without Pretending.* Chicago: Moody, 1973.

Trueblood, Elton. *The Lord's Prayers.* New York: Harper & Row, 1965.

Vigeveno, H. S. *Jesus the Revolutionary.* Glendale, Calif.: Regal, 1966.

Moody Press, a ministry of Moody Bible Institute,
is designed for education, evangelization, and edification.
If we may assist you in knowing more about Christ
and the Christian life, please write us without obligation:
Moody Press, c/o MLM, Chicago, Illinois 60610.